CHRISTIAN METZ
AND THE REALITY OF FILM

This is a volume in the Arno Press Collection

DISSERTATIONS ON FILM 1980

Advisory Editor
Garth S. Jowett

*See last pages of this volume
for a complete list of titles*

CHRISTIAN METZ
AND THE REALITY OF FILM

George Agis Cozyris

ARNO PRESS

A New York Times Company
New York • 1980

Editorial Supervision: Steve Bedney

First publication in book form 1980 by Arno Press Inc.

Copyright © 1980 by George Agis Cozyris

Reproduced by permission of George A. Cozyris

DISSERTATIONS ON FILM 1980
ISBN for complete set: 0-405-12900-9
See last pages of this volume for titles.

Publisher's Note: The text in this book has been reproduced
from the best available copy.

Manufactured in the United States of America

Library of Congress Cataloging in Publication Data

Cozyris, George Agis.
    Christian Metz and the reality of film.

    (Dissertations on film 1980)
    Originally presented as the author's thesis,
University of Southern California, 1979.
    Bibliography: p.
    1. Metz, Christian. Langage et cinéma.
  2. Metz, Christian. Essais sur la signification
au cinéma. 3. Moving-pictures--Philosophy.
I. Title. II. Series.
PN1995.M4523C6 1980   791.43'01'41   79-6670
ISBN 0-405-12904-1

CHRISTIAN METZ AND THE REALITY OF FILM

by

George Agis Cozyris

————————

A Dissertation Presented to the

FACULTY OF THE GRADUATE SCHOOL

UNIVERSITY OF SOUTHERN CALIFORNIA

In Partial Fulfillment of the

Requirements for the Degree

DOCTOR OF PHILOSOPHY

(Communication--Cinema)

January 1979

TO

MY MOTHER AND FATHER

ACKNOWLEDGMENT

I would like to thank the members of my dissertation committee for their help and critical comments. In particular, I wish to express my appreciation to Professor Irwin Blacker for his encouragement and counsel throughout the preparation of this study.

CONTENTS

INTRODUCTION

Statement of the Problem

Christian Metz is considered by many to be one of the most important film theoreticians of our times. Even those who have reservations about the validity of applying to the study of film the principles of structural linguistics, realize that Metz has significantly influenced those who have been trying to develop this new "scientific" approach to film theory and criticism. Certainly, Metz was the first to give to the semiological, structuralist approach in film an aura of seriousness and respectability.

By now it is practically impossible to find any piece of cine-structuralist writing which does not contain some reference to a concept, distinction, or argument which appeared first in Metz's works.

In the manner of a Renaissance "master," Metz even finds himself surrounded by student-disciples who either undertake projects assigned by him, or conduct studies bearing his influence.[1]

An increasing number of books which are offered as textbooks for film courses at colleges and universities not only contain references to Metz, but show very clearly the

1

influence which his writings have had on their authors.[2]

Up to now the world of professional filmmaking has been almost totally indifferent toward the cine-structuralist movement. This has been an approach for studying film, not for making films. However, since Metz claims that his brand of cine-structuralism, the semiology of film, is an attempt to understand how films communicate, one would expect that such an understanding will be utilized eventually in producing films. In that sense, his work can be of a normative nature.

The problem which I tried to deal with in this study was to determine to what extent Christian Metz has contributed something of value toward our understanding of how films communicate; something which goes beyond what we already know about film communication from the writings of the film theoreticians of the conventional, non-semiological, approaches to film theory and criticism.

To deal with this problem I confronted the work of Christian Metz with what I call in this study the "reality of film."

This was done because, although a phenomenon may be studied from a variety of viewpoints and Metz is entitled to choose his viewpoint, one may not distort or pervert the phenomenon to make it fit the viewpoint. This is a fundamental principle of the scientific procedure.

If one claims to be studying how films communicate, one

2

must be studying films. One may not invent something which is not film, study it, and hope to learn how films communicate.

By "film" I mean the feature-length fiction film (what Metz calls the "narrative film") which up to now has been the object of Metz's investigations.

The reality of film, as perceived by me, contains the following elements:

1. A narrative film has an author. Although film-making is a collaborative art, the author of the film is the director who bases his work on the inspiration provided by the screenplay.

2. A narrative film is meant to be screened in a motion picture theatre for the benefit of an audience.

The audience does not have physical access to the print of the film; the audience experiences the film as projected. This experience is usually limited to a single showing of the film although people are free to see a film a number of times.

3. The relationship between a narrative film and its audience is that between a work of art and a group of people experiencing a work of art.

4. The content of a narrative film is an important element in the comprehension, appreciation, and enjoyment of the film.

5. Each individual film is a unique determination on

the level of each shot, and as far as the overall organization of its visual and auditory elements is concerned.
There are no two films which are alike.

6. A narrative film is rooted in a given society and
culture and reflects the period in which it was created.

7. A narrative film nearly always represents a
commercial venture requiring that the film recoup its
production cost and, hopefully, show a profit.

The film theoreticians, critics, and, in general,
"writers" of the conventional, non-semiological approach (all
those dismissed by Metz and his followers as naïve and
sentimental "impressionists"), have been dealing with films
as an audience experiences them at a motion picture
theatre. The questions are, what has Christian Metz been
studying for the past decade and a half? and where does he
differ from those he criticizes?

It is hoped that by confronting his work with the
reality of film we could find suitable answers to the
problem.

Significance of the Study

As the review of the literature and the bibliography
indicate, there have been many studies on Metz's work.
However, to the best of my knowledge, there has never been
a study such as the one attempted here.

A considerable number of the existing studies are
concerned with "internal matters" within the framework of

4

the semiological and cine-semiological movement. They
analyze and argue the appropriateness and validity of Metz's
methods in terms of structural linguistics and semiotics.
In short, they accept his basic premises.

In those studies where concern is shown for Metz's
achievements in terms of our understanding of how films
communicate, there are only a few and scattered references
to the reality of film.

Most of the studies which express approval for Metz's
methods have been written by semiologists like himself, or
by those who have been influenced by him and adopted his
methods. These studies do not appear to be making an
effort to examine closely Metz's methods.

It is mostly in studies which are critical of Metz
that the references to the reality of film can be found.
But, these few and scattered references are made in connection with very specific points raised by Metz, not with his
overall method. Where there are comments about his work as
a whole, they are not sufficiently documented.

The most serious problem with all of the studies which
were located is that they do not deal adequately with
something very fundamental: Is Metz really studying film?
This is a very important question for several reasons.

First, there is a need, an urgent need, to find out
more about how films communicate. Any activity which
honestly claims, or pretends to study film communication,

when in reality it does not, cannot advance or deepen our knowledge and understanding of film as a medium of communication.

Second, Metz's semiological approach has been accepted by many as a major key for unlocking the doors to our understanding of film communication. As a result, countless students in film courses all over the world are struggling with Metz's concepts and they are attempting to use his methods to analyze films. Major periodicals in the area of film scholarship and in other fields have devoted and continue to devote precious space to articles on cine-semiology. Professional meetings and conferences at times become battlegrounds for the cine-structuralists and their opponents.

If Metz is not really studying film, is it not possible that all the activities which his work has generated can be, somehow, harmful to film scholarship?

It seems to me that confronting Metz's work with the reality of film has been long overdue. Unless, perhaps, one can claim that a certain amount of distance, a perspective, was required. Now, more than a decade and a half after Metz started his investigations, perhaps it is the appropriate time to conduct a study such as the one at hand.

Limits of the Study

This study has taken into consideration three works by Christian Metz which are the primary sources. The first

is *Film Language: A Semiotics of the Cinema*.[3] The second is
Language and Cinema.[4] The third work by Metz is his essay "The
Imaginary Signifier."[5]

The choice of *Film Language* and *Language and Cinema* does not
really need to be defended. Although they do not contain
every essay Metz wrote in the 1960s and early 1970s, they
are without doubt the works which contain the essence of his
approach during that decade.

"The Imaginary Signifier" is a different case. It is
one of a number of essays in which Metz has tried to incorporate psychoanalytic concepts and techniques to his already
established semiological approach. "The Imaginary Signifier" is characteristic, I believe, of Metz's current phase;
a phase which is obviously still evolving. As it often
happens in Metz's writings this essay contains references to
his earlier works which he attempts now to relate to his
current psychoanalytic approach.

Since his new approach is still in the process of
evolving, we cannot be very critical of what he is attempting to do. However, there is substantial evidence, which
will be discussed in Chapter V, that Metz is in the process
of doing with the psychoanalytic approach what he did
earlier with the semiological.

In an effort not to lose sight of the goal of this
study, to confront Metz's work with the reality of film, and
in order to avoid the mistakes and weaknesses of previous

studies, I have tried as much as possible not to become involved in the "internal affairs" of the cine-semiologists. That is, I have tried to stay clear of arguments which involve comparisons between the approach of this and that semiologist or linguist.

I have also tried to disentangle Metz's views from those of other authorities in linguistics and in cine-structuralism. This was not an easy task because of the manner in which Metz and his colleagues present their views.

In arguing over a point, there is a tendency of these scholars to invoke one another as an authority on a subject, thus creating a confusing circularity.

When Metz is applying a certain principle borrowed from linguistics or another field, I hold him accountable for it regardless of what a Roland Barthes or a Louis Hjelmslev has to say about it. If one fails to do this, it is practically impossible to move on and to attempt to talk about motion pictures.

Related to the above point is the matter of the semiological and other jargon with which Metz's work is filled. Other than dealing with this problem in Chapter I and Chapter V, as part of Metz's tendency to constantly generate new terms and to revise old ones, I have not attempted in this study to keep track of any sort of evolution of Metz's terminology.

In a number of places in Metz's writings, especially in

Language and Cinema, I encountered passages which appeared to me to be incomprehensible after considerable study. This was obviously a source of great frustration. Only when I came upon references by scholars who pointed out that Metz's thought is characterized by great confusion and obscurity, I consoled myself that there was nothing wrong with my ability to grasp complex semiological ideas.[6]

One of the reasons given by certain members of the editorial board of *Screen* for resigning their positions in 1976 was the obscurity and inaccessibility of the views of those contributing to this "bible" of cine-structuralism and cine-semiology; especially in connection with the new psychoanalytic approach. These former editors of *Screen* spoke of dealing with the contents of the magazine as a torment of endless rereadings in an effort to understand.[7] *Screen* has published a considerable number of Metz's essays as well as analyses of his works.

Upon further inquiry into the writing style of some of Metz's mentors such as Michel Foucault and Jacques Lacan, I came upon references to an intentional obscurity on their part as a matter of strategy.[8]

I am now confident that such gaps in my comprehension of certain passages in Metz's works are not serious enough to undermine any important aspects of this study.

The secondary sources for this study were analyses and evaluations of Metz's work appearing in a variety of periodicals and books.

The majority of these sources presented rather polarized views on the value of Metz's works. The man is either admired or dismissed for wasting our time. For this reason I was very cautious about making use of such secondary sources. In most cases, secondary sources merely provided me with clues as to which aspects of Metz's work needed to be studied more closely in terms of the confrontation with the reality of film.

Since the works by Metz which I decided to use as my primary sources were available in English, I saw no reason to study them in the original French. The translator's notes indicated no unusual problems with the translations despite Metz's style and the subject.

Review of the Literature

The specific works consulted for this study are listed in the Bibliography. Basically, in this review of the literature I want to point out the way I approached the task of acquiring a background in the fields of scholarship on which Christian Metz bases his work. This was a necessary task because without an understanding of the analytic tools which Metz borrows from fields outside cinema it is not possible to deal with his work.

After consulting a number of general works on linguistics, I tried to acquire a background in structural linguistics which is related to semiology in a number of ways.

In the areas of linguistics and structural linguistics I paid particular attention to the writers, such as Louis Hjelmslev, who exerted the greatest influence on Metz.

Although no attempt was made in my study to place Metz in any kind of a perspective within the overall field of literary analysis and criticism, I found it necessary to look into fields such as Russian Formalism, Structuralism, and French New Criticism.

Some of the key objections raised about the validity of certain aspects of structural analysis of literature, especially the most "mechanical" ones, are very similar to the objections which have been raised about Metz's approach to film.

Some of the most useful works which deal with problems in structural analysis of literary works are those by Jameson,[9] Scholes,[10] Segre,[11] and Wetherill.[12]

Wetherill's book provided some interesting insights into the problems involved in connection with Metz's claim that his is a scientific approach to the study of film. The extensive bibliography in Wetherill led me to other interesting works which deal with the subject more thoroughly.

Since there are quite a few phenomenological aspects to Metz's approach, I made an effort to get acquainted with the basic principles of phenomenology and its relationship to art and literary analysis. Interesting works in this area are those of Ihde[13] and Wolf.[14]

Metz's references to the work of Claude Lévi-Strauss and his structural analysis of myths forced me to inquire into Lévi-Strauss and his work. In the extensive literature on Lévi-Strauss a number of works were useful to me because certain features of Strauss' structuralism present problems which are similar to the ones Metz faces. These are the works of Hayes[15] and Rossi.[16]

The dialectical aspects of Metz's method made it necessary for me to look into the subject of dialectics and, to some extent, Marxist aesthetics. In this area the most useful works are those of DeGeorge,[17] Dembo,[18] and Jameson.[19] An exceptionally useful and extensive bibliography on Marxist aesthetics is that of Baxandall.[20]

To deal with Metz's recent efforts to introduce to his semiology the psychology of Sigmund Freud and Jacques Lacan, I consulted a number of works on psychology and psychiatry. Particular emphasis was placed on analyses of those aspects of the work of Freud and Lacan which are utilized by Metz in "The Imaginary Signifier."

Since there are references to Melanie Klein in Metz's essay, a number of her works and several analyses of her writings were consulted.

The most useful of the studies on Lacan, a writer with a particularly difficult style, as those of Miel,[21] Rifflet-Lemaire,[22] Shands,[23] and Wilden.[24]

Repeated references by Metz to Andre Bazin and to other

key theoreticians of the cinema made it necessary for me to read again certain basic texts of the cinematic literature and to relate them to the points which Metz was making. I paid particular attention to those aspects of Bazin's writings which deal with the impression of reality in the cinema.

Outline of the Study

The material in this study is organized in five chapters, a Summary and Conclusions, and a Bibliography.

Chapter I deals with all three of Metz's works. Chapters II, III, and IV deal only with *Film Language* and *Language and Cinema*. Chapter V deals with "The Imaginary Signifier."

The first chapter, entitled "The Tortured Mind," is an examination of Metz's way of approaching his subject; it deals with his methods and his style.

This chapter refers to all three of his works and points out the state of confusion, frustration, tension, and great hesitancy which characterizes his thought.

An attempt is made to describe the circularity of his thought, the ad infinitum fragmentation of every dimension and every element of every dimension he touches upon, the seemingly endless neologisms, and the lack of documentation and evidence which plague his work despite his claim to being "scientific."

This chapter also points out that Metz's approach resembles a game with an infinite number of rules which are modified at any time to suit the purposes of the player.

I felt that such a chapter was necessary because the manner in which Metz thinks and writes is very much related to his inability to deal with the reality of film.

The second chapter, entitled "From Movies to Cine-Text," examines how Metz methodically reduces film to a detached, authorless, and lifeless object. It is this object, and not film, which he proceeds to make the subject of his study.

This chapter points out that Metz ignores the content of films and attempts to deal only with codes, sub-codes, and structures; a process which allows him to engage in very abstract theorizing but which does not permit him to deal with the reality of film.

The third chapter, "Metz and the Film Audience," deals with the place of the film audience in Metz's scheme of things. It attempts to show that the manner in which Metz studies film is almost totally unrelated to those aspects of the reality of film which involve the audience. One of the things which I try to point out in this chapter is that all the mental activity which Metz describes in connection with his codes, sub-codes, and structures, does not describe the experience of an audience viewing a motion picture film, and it is of no value in letting us know how films communicate.

The fourth chapter, "The Severed Roots," looks into the rootless and barren nature of Metz's cine-text when it comes to the social and cultural aspects of the reality of film.

The fifth chapter, "The Imaginary Signifier," deals with the essay which establishes Metz's new psychoanalytic direction. In this chapter, after a brief presentation of the general characteristics and features of this new approach, Metz's attempt to combine structural linguistics with psychoanalysis is examined in terms of the key dimensions of the reality of film.

The Summary and Conclusions is followed by the Bibliography.

Due to the very frequent references to the primary sources, the following abbreviations are used in this study: FL = *Film Language*, LC = *Language and Cinema*, IS = "The Imaginary Signifier."

FOOTNOTES

[1] See Sylvain du Pasquier's "Buster Keaton's Gags,"
Journal of Modern Literature , 3, No. 2 (April, 1973), 269-291.

[2] A good example is James Monaco's *How to Read a Film* (New York: Oxford University Press, 1977).

[3] Christian Metz, *Film Language: A Semiotics of the Cinema*
New York: Oxford University Press, 1974). A collection of
essays originally published in French as *Essais sur la
signification au cinema*. On the occasion of publishing the
collection in English, Metz made a number of revisions and
added footnotes in which he qualified and modified some of
his views. However, this book still represents Metz's
point of view of the early and mid-1960s.

[4] Christian Metz, *Language and Cinema* (The Hague: Mouton,
1974). A translation into English of his *Langage et cinema,*
originally published in French in 1971. It is representa-
tive of Metz's thought in the late 1960s and early 1970s.

[5] Christian Metz, "The Imaginary Signifier," *Screen,* 16,
No. 2 (Summer, 1975), 14-76.

[6] See Brian Henderson, "Metz: 'Essais I' and Film
Theory," *Film Quarterly,* 28, No. 3 (Spring, 1975), 12-33.
Also see Alfred Guzzetti, "Christian Metz and the Semiology
of the Cinema," *Journal of Modern Literature,* 3, No. 2 (April,
1973), 272-308.

[7] Edward Buscombe, Christine Gledhill, Alan Lovell, and
Christopher Williams, "Psychoanalysis and Film," *Screen,* 16,
No. 4 (Winter, 1975/76), 119-130. Also see "Why We Have
Resigned from the Board of *Screen,*" *Screen,* 17, No. 2 (Sum-
mer, 1976), 106-109.

[8] Edward Buscombe, et al., "Psychoanalysis and Film,"
120.

[9] Fredric Jameson, *The Prison-House of Language: A Critical
Account of Structuralism and Russian Formalism* (Princeton, New
Jersey: Princeton University Press, 1972).

[10] Robert Scholes, *Structuralism in Literature* (New Haven:
Yale University Press, 1974).

[11] Cesare Segre, *Semiotics and Literary Criticism* (The Hague:
Mouton, 1973).

[12]P. M. Wetherill, *The Literary Text: An Examination of Critical Methods* (Oxford: Basil Blackwell, 1974).

[13]Don Ihde, *Hermeneutic Phenomenology* (Evanston: Northwestern University Press, 1971).

[14]Janet Wolff, *Hermeneutic Philosophy and the Sociology of Art* (London: Routledge & Paul, 1975).

[15]E. Nelson Hayes and Tanya Hayes, eds., *Claude Lévi-Strauss: The Anthropologist as Hero* (Cambridge: The Massachusetts Institute of Technology Press, 1970).

[16]Ino Rossi, ed., *The Unconscious in Culture: The Structuralism of Claude Lévi-Strauss in Perspective* (New York: E. P. Dutton & Co., 1974).

[17]Richard T. DeGeorge and M. Fernande, eds., *The Structuralists from Marx to Lévi-Strauss* (Garden City, N. Y.: Anchor Books, 1972).

[18]L. S. Dembo, ed., *Criticism: Speculative and Analytical Essays* (Madison, Milwaukee: The University of Wisconsin Press, 1967).

[19]Fredric Jameson, *Marxism and Form: Twentieth-Century Dialectical Theories of Criticism* (Princeton: Princeton University Press, 1972).

[20]Lee Bauxandall, comp., *Marxism and Aesthetics: A Selective Annotated Bibliography; Books and Articles in the English Language* (New York: Humanities Press, 1968).

[21]Jan Miel, *Jacques Lacan and the Structure of the Unconscious*, Yale French Studies, Nos. 36-37 (New Haven: Yale University Press, 1966), pp. 104-111.

[22]A. Rifflet-Lemaire, *Jacques Lacan* (Brussels: Dessart, 1970).

[23]Harley C. Shands, "Semiotic Approaches to Psychiatry," *Approaches to Semiotics,* ed. T. A. Sebeok (The Hague: Mouton, 1970), pp. 170-187.

[24]Anthony Wilden, "Freud, Signorelli, and Lacan: The Repression of the Signifier," *American Imago,* 23, No. 4 (Winter, 1966), 332-366.

CHAPTER I

THE TORTURED MIND

This chapter deals with certain aspects and features of Metz's methodology and style which serve as useful background information in the investigation of how his work is related to the reality of film.

The Reasons for Metz's "Intervention"

As one of the pioneers and main spokesmen for the cine-structuralist movement, Christian Metz has been quite critical of the conventional, non-structuralist approach to film theory and criticism.

Film Language, Language and Cinema, "The Imaginary Signifier," and practically everything else he has written, contain numerous references to the inadequacy of the conventional approach. His criticism usually takes the form of dismissing in a condescending manner most of the writings of film theoreticians appearing before his "intervention" in the early 1960s. When he does give credit to contributions he considers useful, he places them within a historical perspective; they were contributions which had some value during the era in which they were made.[1]

However, Metz has been kind enough to express his willingness to "forgive the cinema of the past for its excesses, because it has given us Eisenstein and a few others. But one always excuses genius" (FL, p. 56).

What Metz finds wrong with the conventional approach is what all the cine-structuralists object to: film has not been studied systematically and scientifically.

Until Metz and his fellow "scientists" came to the rescue, it is said, film theory and criticism were basically an impressionistic account of a critic's response to films. There was no critical method with a deductive analytic and evaluative apparatus. Dialogue between theoreticians and critics was an exchange of rival assertions. There was a failure to distinguish between evaluation and description. A subjectivism, humanism, and moralism undermined most theories and approaches to the cinema. Classical film aesthetics posited a unity and a coherence to every work which required that a search be made through the content of films to discover a "message." Marxist cine-structuralists even suggested that conventional film theory is part of the "conspiracy" of the bourgeois capitalist society to force the oppressed masses to accept the "reality" of an unjust social system.[2]

To all of the above reasons for rejecting the conventional approach, Metz added one which according to him was quite important: the time had come for a new era.

Obviously echoing the manner and style of Ferdinand de Saussure, who in the early 1900s announced that the new science of semiotics had the right to exist,[3] Metz in the 1960s heralded in *Film Language* that "The time has come for a semiotics of the cinema" (FL, p. 91).

However, for something as important as the end of an era and the dawning of a new one featuring a new science, Metz provided no reason other than his feeling that it had to be so. The "old" film theory was declared to have contributed whatever it had to contribute and it had to go.[4]

Half a decade after that triumphant announcement, and after exhaustive investigations on his part, in the Conclusion to his *Language and Cinema,* Metz made another proclamation: ". . . the semiotics of the cinema does not yet exist." (LC, p. 287). It is also interesting to note that soon after that proclamation Metz turned toward a new hope for the proper study of film: psychoanalysis.

The structural linguistic approach which Metz applies to film theory has as its purpose to accomplish in the field of cinema ". . . the great Saussurian dream of studying the mechanisms by which human significations are transmitted in human society" (FL, p. 91).

Because Metz feels that the fiction film, the "narrative film" as he calls it, has assumed a social superiority over other types of film, he applies his structural linguistic approach to this type of film only.

In *Language and Cinema,* Metz points out that

> the semiotician finds before him the already realized film. He
> thus has nothing to say about how it ought to be made . . . He is
> concerned with seeing how the film is constructed . . . The
> semiotician . . . would also like to be able to understand how
> the film is understood. (LC, pp. 73-74)

Halfway through *Language and Cinema*, he points out that
the task of the semiotics of what he calls the "filmic fact"
is "to analyze film texts in order to discover either
textual systems, cinematic codes, or sub-codes" (LC,
p. 150). He hopes that these elements within the "filmic
fact" will enable him to understand how films communicate.

In "The Imaginary Signifier," Metz describes in this
manner the new psychoanalytic approach to the study of film:

> To sum up, what I have analyzed, or attempted to analyse, in my
> first two Freudian inspired studies . . . turns out, without
> having precisely intended it, to be already established on one
> of the flanks of the ridge-line, that of the imaginary: cine-
> matic fiction as a semioneiric instance, in one of these
> articles, and in the other, the spectator-screen relationship as
> a mirror identification. That is why I should now like to
> approach my subject from the symbolic flank, or rather along the
> ridge-line itself. My dream today is to speak of the cinematic
> dream in terms of a code: of the code of this dream. (IS,
> p. 18)

His introduction of psychoanalysis in the study of film
is justified in "The Imaginary Signifier" by saying that
"linguistics and psychology are the two main 'sources' of
semiology, the only disciplines that are semiotic through
and through" (IS, p. 28). As it happened earlier with his
heralding of a new era of the semiotics of the cinema, in
this essay a new hope is expressed and a new dawn is
predicted. He now says that the semiotics of the cinema

21

will become possible through a combination of structural
linguistics and psychoanalysis.

Metz's Awareness of the Reality of Film

It is important to point out that Metz appears to be
very much aware of the reality of film. This is clearly
evident in the primary sources used for this study and I
want to quote Metz rather extensively.

In *Film Language,* Metz indicates his awareness of the
reality of film in a variety of ways. On the impression of
reality upon the spectator he says:

> Films give us the feeling that we are witnessing an almost real
> spectacle. . . . Films release a mechanism of affective and
> perceptual participation in the spectator . . . they speak to
> us with the accents of true evidence, using the argument that
> "it is so." (FL, p. 4)

> The reason why cinema can bridge the gap between true art and
> the general public . . . is that films have the appeal of a
> presence and of a proximity that strikes the masses and fills
> the movie theatres. This phenomenon, which is related to the
> impression of reality, is naturally of great aesthetic
> significance. (FL, p. 5)

He identifies movement and the dimension of time as key
elements for the vivid impression of reality:

> . . . why the impression of reality is so much more vivid in a
> film than it is in a photograph . . . ? An answer immediately
> suggests itself: It is movement . . . that produces the strong
> impression of reality. (FL, p. 7)

> Before the cinema, there was photography . . . But, accurate
> as it was, this means was still not sufficiently lifelike: It
> lacked the dimension of time; it could not render volume
> acceptably. (FL, p. 14)

Through repeated references to the theatrical and
narrative nature of the fiction film he admits that story-

telling is an important element of the reality of film:

> The basic formula, which has never changed, is the one that consists in making a large continuous unit that tells a story and calling it a "movie." . . . Going to the movies is going to see this type of story. . . . The rule of the "story" is so powerful that the image, which is said to be the major constituent of film, vanishes behind the plot it has woven. (FL, p. 45)

> All one retains of a film is its plot and a few images. Daily experience confirms this. (FL, p. 46)

> It is difficult to see how the cinema can ever become truly "non-theatrical." (FL, p. 191)

> Remove "drama," and there is no fiction, no diegesis, and therefore no film. (FL, p. 194)

> To exclude the dimension of the scenario from the modern cinema, or to belittle it, is like saying that the only scenarios are those that are like the scripts of Aurenche and Bost. (FL, p. 203)

Metz admits that film is an art and that it started developing along the lines of an art very early:

> From the very beginning, threatened with extinction, it became an art. (FL, p. 58)

As an art, film possesses the qualities of uniqueness and one-way communication:

> Every image is a *hapax* [a unique determination]. (FL, p. 69)

> Now, like all the arts, and because it is itself an art, the cinema is one-way communication. (FL, p. 75)

The poetic and "language of art" dimensions of film are mentioned by Metz a number of times:

> Resembling true languages as it does, film, with its superior instancy, is of necessity projected "upward" into the sphere of art--where it reverts to a specific language. The film total can only be a language if it is already an art. (FL, 58)

> In point of fact, the cinema is not a language but a language of art. (FL, p. 64)

23

One will have to recognize that the cinematographic enterprise, whether successful or not, is initially poetic. (FL, p. 204)

Metz knows that, being an art, film can only give the impression that it renders the external world as it really is. He says:

A film is never objective. (FL, p. 195)

When it comes to the sociocultural roots of the cinema, Metz demonstrates a very clear understanding of what is involved in terms of this aspect of the reality of film:

There remains, of course, a problem, and that is that cinemato-graphic language itself, in as it is a body of orderings, must certainly be influenced by various sociocultural codifications . . . the types of filmic ordering must in one way or another refer to given patterns of intelligibility within society. (FL, p. 215)

Important elements of the sociocultural influences evident in film are, according to Metz, various kinds of "censorships";

The mutilation of the content of films is frequently the pure and simple result of political censorship . . . More frequently still, it is the result of commercial censorship . . . a true economic censorship . . . so that in the cinema the problems of content are linked to external permission much more than in the other arts. (FL, p. 236)

An interesting kind of "censorship" which Metz calls "The Plausible," is related to the kind of stories and other expressive elements in films which are present or absent as a result of pressures brought upon the filmmakers by the social conditioning of the audiences:

The Plausible, I said, is cultural and arbitrary: I mean that the line of division between the possibilities it excludes and those it retains (and even promotes socially) varies considerably according to the country, the period, the art, and the genre. (FL, p. 244)

24

The admission that, as cultural objects, films reflect one another, is another way by which Metz indicates his awareness of the reality of film:

> Since the film-maker shoots films, to some degree he often shoots the films of other people, believing that he is shooting his own. To tear oneself away, even partially, from an attraction so profoundly rooted in the very fact of culture, in the shape of fields, requires unusual strength of mind. Books reflect each other; so do paintings, and so do films. (FL, p. 245)

In *Language and Cinema* there are numerous indications that Metz is well aware of the reality of film.

He admits that film is an art:

> It is equally clear that the study of film is of interest to aesthetics: the film is always a "work of art." (LC, p. 15)

> The complexity of films is also the result of the fact that the cinema is what we call an art. (LC, p. 37)

Film is an art because of its social status and function:

> We will maintain only that the film--and even the ugliest, dullest, and most obscure one--is always a work of art by virtue of its social status. (LC, p. 38)

> The film is a work of art by its intention. . . . It is also a work of art by its consumption . . . The cinema is an art because it functions socially as such. (LC, p. 38)

As works of art, films are unique systems of expressive elements:

> Each film has its own structure, which is an organized whole, a fabric in which everything fits together; in short a system. But this system is valid only for one film. . . . To the extent that films are considered as unique totalities, each contains within itself a system which is as unique as the film itself. (LC, p. 63)

The sociocultural dimension of film is admitted by Metz a number of times:

> What is referred to globally as "cinema" (and to a lesser degree as "film") is, in reality, a vast and complex socio-cultural phenomenon, a sort of total social fact . . . which includes, as is well known, important economic and financial elements. (LC, p. 9)

> But today the cinema, although a recent development as noted above, has become an established cultural fact. (LC, p. 10)

> A film, in other words, is not only an example of cinema, but also a culture. (LC, p. 72)

As cultural objects films contain reflections of the society in which they are produced and "consumed":

> It is common occurrence that films, consciously or not, reflect various systems of political thought. (LC, p. 99)

> The film reflects social behavior, but may also remodel it to a certain extent. (LC, p. 116)

In "The Imaginary Signifier" there are quite a few indications that Metz is aware of the reality of film. Most of them reflect Metz's marxist orientation, but they are still indications of an awareness of this reality:

> It has very often, and right, been said that the cinema is a technique of the imaginary. A technique, on the other hand, which is peculiar to a historical epoch (that of capitalism) and a state of society, so-called industrial civilization. (IS, p. 15)

> Let me insist once again, the cinematic institution is not just the cinema industry . . . it is also the mental machinery--another industry--which spectators "accustomed to the cinema" have internalized historically and which has adapted them to the consumption of films. (IS, pp. 18-19)

Metz knows well that films are not abstract linguistic entities but popular entertainment presented for the enjoyment of a fee-paying audience:

> The cinema is attended out of desire, not reluctance, in the hope that the film will please, not that it will displease. (IS, p. 19)

26

The "desire to go to the cinema" is a kind of reflection shaped by the film industry, but it is also a real link in the chain of the overall mechanism of that industry. It occupies one of the essential positions in the circulation of money, the turnover of capital without which films could no longer be made. (IS, p. 19)

If I am concerned to define the cinematic institution as a wider instance than the cinema industry . . . it is because of this dual kinship . . . between the psychology of the spectator . . . and the final mechanisms of the cinema. (IS, p. 20)

While discussing the traditions from which the cinema has drawn its expressive means, Metz admits again that film is an art deeply rooted in western culture:

Since its birth at the end of the nineteenth century the cinema has, as it were, been snapped up by the Western, Aristotelian tradition of the fictional and representational arts, of diegesis and mimesis, for which its spectators were prepared--prepared in spirit, but also instinctively--by their experience of the novel, of theatre, of figurative painting, and which was thus the most profitable tradition for the film industry. (IS, p. 44)

With such an awareness of the reality of film, one cannot help but wonder why and how could Metz fail to deal with this reality in his effort to study how films communicate.

Building on Vagueness, Uncertainty, and Hesitancy

For someone setting out to create a new science, the semiotics of the cinema, Metz has the right to be cautious. In *Film Language* he takes great pains to develop very slowly his concepts; especially that of cinematic narrativity. Very large sections of *Language and Cinema* are devoted to a painstaking clearing of the ground for the establishment of what he calls the "cinematic codes" and the "distinctive units." In "The Imaginary Signifier" it takes Metz fourteen pages (out of the sixty-three page essay) to state why he is interested in a psychoanalytic approach to film, and then another eighteen pages for him to indicate what the subject of this essay is going to be.

However, there is a difference between a slow, deliberate, and methodical approach, which is based on solid ground, and an approach which is based on methodical vagueness, uncertainty, and hesitancy.

In *Film Language*, where he is setting the foundations of his cine-semiology, Metz declares that "I am persuaded on the contrary that the 'filmolinguistic' venture is entirely justified, and that it must be fully 'linguistic'--that is to say, solidly based on linguistics itself" (FL, p. 60).

He then proceeds in a very efficient manner to discover not the ways in which the cinema is like a language which can be studied through linguistics, but to discover the many ways in which the cinema is *not* like a language.

By his own admission, the cinema differs from language in the following fundamental ways:

> There is nothing in the cinema that corresponds, even metaphorically, to the second articulation. (FL, p. 61)

> The cinema has no phonemes; nor does it, whatever one may say, have words. Except on occasion, and more or less by chance, it is not subject to the first articulation. (FL, p. 65)

> There is no precise syntax in the cinema in the proper linguistic sense of the term "syntax." (FL, pp. 67-68)

> There are many characteristics to the filmic image that distinguish it from the preferred form of signs--which is arbitrary, conventional, and codified. (FL, p. 76)

28

The paradigmatic category in film is practically non-existent.
(FL, pp. 68-69, 101)

The cinema is not a language system, because it contradicts three
important characteristics of the linguistic fact: a language is
a system of signs used for inter-communication . . . Now, like
all the arts, and because it is itself an art, the cinema is one-
way communication. (FL, p. 75)

In the cinema connotation is nothing other than a form of
denotation. (FL, p. 118)

I would say, on the contrary, that the cinema has never had a
grammar. (FL, p. 209)

While he is discovering that cinema is not like a
language, Metz begins to attribute to this entity the characteristics of a language so that he can proceed anyway and
study it using an approach which is solidly based on
linguistics itself.

In this procedure, the man who intervened in the
course of film theory to do away with "impressionism," makes
statements such as these:

[Cinema] "resembles true languages." (FL, p. 58)

[The image] "corresponds to one or more sencences." (FL, p. 65)

There is a syntax of the cinema, but it remains to be made. (FL,
p. 67)

The image is a form of speech. (FL, p. 67)

Thus a kind of filmic articulation appears. (FL, p. 99)

The cinema is certainly not a language system (langue). It can,
however, be considered as a language. (FL, p. 105)

Although it lacks distinctive signifying units, film proceeds by
whole "blocks of reality," which are actualized with their total
meaning of discourse. (FL, p. 115)

These "blocks of reality" bring about "a kind of
articulation."

> All that can be affirmed, therefore, is that a shot is less
> unlike a statement than a word but it does not necessarily
> resemble a statement. (FL, p. 116)

In the middle of this process of attempting somehow to
relate film to language, Metz apparently senses that he can
no longer sustain his earlier dogmatism, and he declares
that "the concepts of linguistics can be applied to the
semiotics of the cinema only with the greatest caution"
(FL, p. 107).

But the problems created by the effort to treat film as
if it were a language, when he knows very well that film
differs fundamentally from a language, overwhelm him and a
general and pervading uncertainty, timidity, and hesitancy
undermines practically everything he is trying to say and
to establish in *Film Language*. Metz's writing contains every
indication that he does not have the situation under
control. Here is a sample of the manner in which he
expresses his thoughts:

> "It is reasonable to think" (FL, p. 7). "One might add" (IS,
> p. 10). "Let us say, therefore--perhaps a little cavalierly--"
> (FL, p. 17). "One can perhaps explain" (FL, p. 19). "We all
> assume" (FL, p. 19). "Nevertheless--aside from the fact that
> the distinction I am suggesting here is, in more than one case,
> extremely difficult to maintain . . . it seems to me" (FL, p. 27).
> "Let us indeed suppose that in certain circumstances a shot can
> appear to be equivalent to several sentences" (FL, p. 66). "One
> can of course conclude that the cinema is not a language" (FL,
> p 89). "It is not possible here to give this table in its com-
> plete form . . . let us content ourselves, then, with the almost
> unpolished 'result'" (FL, p. 119). "On a level roughly corre-
> sponding to that of the 'sequence'" (FL, p. 120). "We are told
> nothing, yet we are informed that a great deal could be told us"
> (FL, p. 132). These three reasons might eventually compel us to
> revise the status (FL, p. 133). It is impossible to locate pre-
> cisely the threshold separating elements we call "large" from
> those we call "small" . . . and yet, however uncertain its

location, the existence of the threshold . . . is beyond doubt (FL, pp. 140-141). A truth that is extremely difficult to define, but that, somehow, one places instinctively (FL, p. 197). The filmic laws are most probably located far beyond the place one usually expects to find them--that is to say, on a much deeper level, a level in some ways prior to the differentiation of verbal language . . . from other human semiotic systems (FL, p. 209).

In *Film Language,* Metz's inability to make any statement without undermining it by repeated and lengthy qualifications, admissions of inconsistencies, and references to hopes for improvement in the future, extends even to his footnotes which are, at times, much longer and more complex than his text.

The same uncertainty and hesitancy is present in *Language and Cinema* and it is expressed through figures of speech very similar to those used in *Film Language.* In *Language and Cinema* one of the best examples of his hesitancy and confusion appears when he is discussing the "code of montage." After he presents a fairly elaborate case for the existence of such a code, he concludes: "Of course, strictly speaking there is no code of montage" (LC, p. 140). Five lines of text later he reverses himself: "But in another sense there is a code of montage." Four lines later he says: "In the extreme and perhaps by forcing things a little, one could conceive of a particular type of code" (LC, p. 140).

In *Language and Cinema,* the position that the semiotics of the cinema can be based solidly on linguistics is abandoned. Now Metz believes that ". . . a semiotic analysis

31

inevitably encounters sociology, cultural history, aesthetics, psychoanalysis, etc." (LC, p. 16). As it has been
mentioned already, *Language and Cinema* ends with the conclusion
that the semiotics of the cinema does not yet exist.
Between the statement on page sixteen and the disturbing
conclusion, Metz does not deal with cine-semiology in terms
of sociology, cultural history, aesthetics, or psychoanalysis. He continues in the vein of *Film Language* but in a much
more technical and detailed fashion. This highly technical
approach is characterized by what appears to be a certain
degree of self-confidence. However, this is not real self-
confidence but the freedom which he has granted to himself
to do and to say whatever he pleases. Barely under the
surface is the same lack of certainty which characterizes
his work in *Film Language*.

Neologisms, Levels, and Ranks

One of the most disturbing qualities of Metz's approach
and style is his practice of coining new terms every time he
discovers that he cannot deal adequately with those which
are already available. *Film Language* and *Language and Cinema*
are filled with Metz's neologisms. Some examples of the
terms created by him are the following:

In *Film Language*: "Straightforward Spatiotemporal
Break." This is what has been known in film as a "Fade."
"Spatiotemporal Break with an Underlying Transitive Link."

In the language of the discredited "impressionistic" film theory this is known as a "Dissolve." "Alternate Syntagma," "Alternating Syntagma," "Frequentative Syntagma," "Full Frequentative Syntagma," "Bracket Frequentative Syntagma," "Semi-Frequentative Syntagma," "Nondiegetic Insert," "Displaced Diegetic Insert," "Extracinematographic," etc.

In *Language and Cinema*: "Cinematic Non-Filmic," "Absolute Film," "General Cinematic Codes," "Partial Cinematic Codes," "The Cinema-Fact," "Singular System," "Cinematization," "Filmization," "Opposing Irredentism," "Global Text," "Syntagm-Token," "Remote Co-presence," "Paradigm-Token," "Mode of Cinematicity," "Suprasegmental Distinctive Units," "Plurifilmic Textual System," "Heterogenous Simultaneous Syntagm," "Homogenous Temporal Syntagm," "Intermixed Specificities," "Metaparadigms," "Meta-Syntagms," "Oblique Syntagms."

In "The Imaginary Signifier": "Sanctioning Construction," "Juxtastructure," "Circumstantial Denotation," "Significatory Pressure," "Manifest Filmic Material," "Proximate Signification," "Great Global Signified," "Super Genres," "Great Cinematic Regimes," "Referential Illusion," "Cinematic Scopic Regime," "Cinematic Voyeurism," "Cinematic Scopophilia," "Cinematic Fetishism."

Newly coined terminology can be troublesome. What makes Metz's creations particularly disturbing is that most of these new terms identify either relationships between entities which Metz does not describe clearly, or they are labels for items which belong to classification systems which, with one exception, are never developed or explained fully.

As far as classification systems are concerned, most of the time Metz creates rung after rung for ladders which he never constructs. The one classification system which he describes in some detail is in *Film Language* and he labels it "The General Table of the Large Syntagmatic Category of the Image-Track."

But even this *Grande Syntagmatique*, supposedly the crowning achievement of his *Film Language*, is nothing more than a presentation in linguistic jargon of types of shots and of relationships between shots which have been discussed in the works of the "conventional" theoreticians of the cinema decades before Metz's "intervention."[5]

For example, a "displaced diegetic insert" is, by Metz's own example, nothing more than a single shot of the pursued in a sequence of shots showing the pursuers (FL, p. 128).

And his "parallel syntagma" is none other than the familiar parallel montage sequence.

The value of the *Grande Syntagmatique* is further undermined by Metz himself when, attempting to praise Jean-Luc Goddard, he discovers that Goddard is using in one of his films a novel kind of syntagma (Metz calls it a "potential sequence") which the *Grande Syntagmatique* cannot account for

(FL, pp. 217-220).

The Impossible Distinctions

Related to the tendency to coin new terms and to
create category after category of items which fit in a
model of the whole which is never presented,[6] is Metz's
habit of creating a great number of distinctions so that
there is hardly a paragraph or a page in *Film Language* and in
Language and Cinema that does not contain some attempted
distinction. The problem with these distinctions is not so
much their number and the fact that they appear with such
frequency that there is no way for someone to reflect
adequately on what is being said; what is really disturbing
is that Metz is unable to establish that there is a difference between the items he attempts to differentiate.

Some examples of these attempted distinctions, with
brief comments, are the following:

In *Film Language*

Image--Simple Description--Narrative (FL, p. 18). Metz
gives examples to illustrate the difference between these
three items: IMAGE: "A motionless and isolated shot of a
stretch of desert . . . (space-significate--space-signi-
fier)." SIMPLE DESCRIPTION: "Several partial and successive shots of the desert waste . . . (space-significate--
time-signifier)." NARRATIVE: "Several successive shots of
a caravan moving across the desert . . . (time-significate--
time-signifier)."

35

Distinctions of this kind generate a lot of very disturbing questions: What does he mean by a "motionless shot?" A static-camera shot? A freeze-frame? A "still nature" shot without a human element in it? Can a motion picture shot exist which does not contain the "time signifier" element? What is the important difference between the shots making up a "simple description" and a "narrative?" The moving caravan? In that case, is the human element what distinguishes "description" from "narrative?" Why is not Metz's "narrative" a "description?" Why is not his "description" a "narrative?" Why is the element of space-significate absent from what he defines as a "narrative?"

Semiotics of Connotation--Semiotics of Denotation (FL, p. 96). Metz attempts to distinguish between these two types of approaches, and he indicates that he will study the semiotics of denotation. However, he is unable to make a clear distinction between these two because of that aspect of the reality of film which involves the impression of reality captured by the image.

In a motion picture shot (in the image) connotation and denotation fuse and Metz admits this a number of times. Finally, he is forced to say that connotation and denotation have "a common root in the actual perception of the spectators" (FL, p. 114). Then he has to invent new distinctions in order to proceed:

This is why, provisionally, I use the term *iconography* to designate the prefilmic connotations of objects, in order to distinguish them from—and at the same time draw them close to—the *iconology* (likewise prefilmic) that organizes the denotation of these same objects. (FL, p. 114)

A few pages later, Metz admits very openly that "in the cinema, even more than elsewhere, connotation is nothing other than a form of denotation" (FL, p. 118).

His inability here to distinguish between connotation and denotation is a very serious matter because he proceeds anyway to take an approach which favors denotation, and this prevents him from focusing properly the subject of his investigation. Since, by his own admission, it is the reality of film which prevents a distinction from being made between connotation and denotation, Metz cannot be blamed for failing to make the distinction. His error is that he attempts to go against the reality of film and, as a result, he has to create a great number of other unreal distinctions in order to proceed with his task.

Visual--Photographic Elements (FL, 106). Metz attempts to distinguish between "visual" and "photographic" elements in film. By way of example he indicates that fades and dissolves are visual but not photographic.

How can a valid distinction be made between these two? Under what kind of logic can a dissolve or a fade in motion pictures be visual and not photographic?

In Metz's writings such obscure distinctions open up new territories of problems, which require more obscure

37

distinctions which create new problems, ad inifinitum.

Minimum Segment--Autonomous Segment (FL, p. 124). Metz
has barely presented this distinction when he points out
that "This, as we will see shortly, does not prevent a
minimum segment from being occasionally autonomous" (FL,
p. 124).

There is pattern in Metz's writings, described in more
detail later on in this chapter under "Circularity," where he
works very diligently to make a distinction or to establish
the validity of something, and then he proceeds to undermine
it by saying that it is not valid.

Location of the Signifier--Location of the Significate
(FL, p. 127). Metz points out that "The screen is the
location of the signifier, and the diegesis is the location
of the significate" (FL, p. 127).

In what sense is the screen the location of the
signifier or anything else? Is the screen really the
location or the mind of the spectator? Metz gives the
impression that he is referring literally to the projection
surface, the screen, as the location of the signifier. Why
is not the diegesis "located" on the screen since what is
"diegesized" appears on the screen? How is it possible to
distinguish between the location of the signifier and the
location of the signified when it has been impossible to
distinguish between the signifier and the signified?

38

Ordinary--Episodic Sequence (FL, p. 130). Inside what
Metz calls the "sequence proper," further described by him
as a "single, discontinuous temporal order," he distinguishes between an "ordinary sequence" and an "episodic
sequence" (FL, p. 130).

For him the "ordinary sequence" is one where the
temporal discontinuity is unorganized. The "episodic
sequence" is one where the temporal discontinuity is
organized.

What is, may we ask, an unorganized temporal discontinuity, or an organized temporal discontinuity? And why
call the first one "ordinary" and the second "episodic?"

In *Language and Cinema*

This book is also filled with very troublesome
distinctions. This is a brief sample of these distinctions:

Cinematic Fact--Filmic Fact. The distinction between
what is cinematic and what is filmic is a major one, and
it is related to Metz's effort to limit his study. It is
also a very important distinction because, as we shall see,
it becomes the source of very serious problems in terms
of the reality of film.

In his usual style, Metz defines things gradually. He
starts by pointing out that:

> Film is only a small part of the cinema, for the later represents
> a vast ensemble of phenomena some of which intervene before the
> film . . . [some] after the film . . . [some] during the film
> . . . [some] aside from and outside of it.

. . . .

> The importance of making this distinction between the cinematic
> and the filmic fact lies in the fact that it allows us to
> restrict the meaning of the term "film" to a more manageable,
> specifiable signifying discourse, in contrast with "cinema"
> which, as defined here, constitutes a larger complex (at whose
> center, however, three predominant dimensions may be distin-
> guished: the technological, the economic, and the sociological).
> (LC, p. 12)

Since Metz's interest lies with the semiotics of the

cinema, he observes that

> It is clear that the so-called semiotics of the cinema is
> primarily concerned with the "filmic fact." In spite of
> inevitable areas of overlap, the semiotics of the cinema cannot
> usefully contribute to the understanding of the "cinematic fact,"
> at least not in any direct manner, and cannot at the present
> stage of research. Semiotics, whether of the film or anything
> else, is the study of discourses and texts.
> . . . .
> Suffice to say that what we shall call "film," except where
> otherwise indicated, is film as a signifying discourse (text),
> or as a linguistic object: Cohen-Séat's filmic fact . . . the
> film functioning as an object perceived by the audience for the
> duration of the projection. It is the "filmophanic" film, and
> it alone, that we shall call "film." (LC, p. 13)

In terms of the reality of film the above comments

about the "filmophanic" film are very important.[7] Their

importance begins to emerge more clearly as we follow what

else Metz has to say in this section of *Language and Cinema*.

His text is being compressed to leave out his usual

complicated digressions and references to hopes for

improvement of his technique in the future:

> 1. The notion of filmic fact . . . is, however, still too vast
>   to attribute to it the principle of analytic distinctiveness
>   suitable to a semiotics of the film, for the film itself is
>   a multi-dimensional phenomenon. (LC, 14).

> 2. It would be tempting to say . . . that within the filmic fact
>   itself, two or three types of phenomena may be isolated--for
>   example, the psychological, sociological, and aesthetic--which

are not of direct concern to semiotics, and which should
therefore be restricted to the study of film considered
as a language system.
. . . .

To this extent, the semiotics of film is inextricably tied
to "psychological" considerations . . . utilized in a different perspective.
. . . .

In this way, a semiotic analysis inevitably encounters
sociology, cultural history, aesthetics, psychoanalysis,
etc. (LC, p. 16)

3. . . . film . . . is a mode of expression in which language
and art maintain a quasi-consubstantial relation to one
another and where language itself is a product or an aspect
of artistic invention.
. . . .

A semiotic analysis is thus closely associated with the
aesthetics of film. (LC, pp. 16-17)

Metz has barely completed his comments about the filmic

fact and the differences between the filmic and the cine-

matic when he makes the following observations:

"Cinema," in fact, is not always (as it is for Cohen-Séat) the
sum of that which is related to the film but external to it;
even at the heart of a filmic analysis cinema continues to be
a notion which intrudes itself at every turn, and which is
hard to imagine doing without.
. . . .

And it is clear, although paradoxical, that the cinema thus
conceived is situated within what Cohen-Séat calls the filmic
fact. (LC, p. 22)

Later on in *Language and Cinema*, Metz writes:

There is something which nevertheless should be called to the
reader's attention: the distinction between the cinematic and
the filmic, which everyday language maintains for better or
worse (obstinately and confusedly at the same time) and which
we would like to make explicit here, does not prevent, in
certain propositions, cinema and film (cinematic and filmic)
from becoming interchangeable and from being spontaneously
felt as such in writing. (LC, p. 55)

As if this were not enough of an admission that he has

failed to make the distinction between "cinema" and "film,"

he repeats:

> The contexts in which "cinema" and "film" (or "cinematic" and "filmic") become interchangeable are quite numerous. (LC, p. 56)

However, in the remaining nine chapters of *Language and Cinema*, Metz acts as if the distinction between "film" and "cinema" has been made successfully, and he develops his analytic procedures so that he leaves out the "cinematic." Also, no matter what Metz says about aesthetic, psychological and socio-cultural dimensions of the "filmic," in the remaining nine chapters he does not deal at all with these dimensions.

Code--Message. All the distinctions and all the analytic elements which are associated with the concept of the "code" are of great importance to Metz because of the central position which the concept of the "code" occupies in his work. For this reason it is quite disturbing to find a distinction such as this:

> Code always differs from message in that one is code and the other message, and--even if the complete list of what one finds in the message were identical with the total list of what one introduces into the code . . . it would still be true that these traits should be understood in the future as being associated with one another throughout a given discourse, and thus linked by the coherence of a logic which is always tacit. (LC, p. 59)

However, he has never attempted to give examples from actual motion picture films to illustrate the difference between message and code.

General--Particular Cinematic Codes. Metz makes a determined effort to distinguish between "general" and

42

"particular" cinematic codes. As this effort reaches its

conclusion he declares:

> The distinction between "general" and "particular" cinematic codes
> is somewhat crude, and fails to account for different degrees of
> generality which a cinematic code may represent. (LC, p. 79)

On the next page Metz continues:

> It should be understood, then, that the so-called "particular"
> codes are codes which are more or less particular--and, from
> this, that the dual division of general and particular codes has
> as its only effect (and also its only goal) to distinguish clearly
> from all others those cinematic systems which present the maximum
> degree of generality. (LC, p. 80)

The Drifting Point of View

As a "scientist" Metz has the right to shift his point

of view as he proceeds with his investigation. Viewing

one's subject from a number of viewpoints can be used as a

safeguard against errors in observation and experimentation.

However, Metz does not merely change his point of view

from time to time and according to some plan which becomes

apparent to us. His is a continuously shifting, drifting

point of view following a pattern which he seems to be .....

making up as he goes along. This disturbing situation is

evident in all his writings and it is especially obvious in

Language and Cinema.

Since this practice is a matter of Metz's overall style

and approach, it is not possible here to quote all the

passages where it occurs. Instead, an attempt is made here

to isolate what causes him to do this and to point out the

consequences of this practice.

There seem to be the following reasons for Metz's

43

drifting point of view:

1. Metz assigns to himself an impossible task which prevents him from focusing properly on the subject of his study. He wants to assume a scientific approach although he is dealing with cinema which, by his own admission, is an art.

He wants to base his approach solidly on linguistics although he realizes that the cinema is not a language.

He attempts to deal with cinema in terms of semiotics although in *Film Language* he admits that the semiotics of the cinema do not exist yet but merely have the right to exist, and in *Language and Cinema* he admits that the semiotics of the cinema do not exist yet.

As a result Metz is forced to take an extremely abstract and theoretical approach containing difficulties which he cannot overcome. Good examples of this are his inability to overcome the problems created by the reality of the image, which causes a fusion between signifier and signified, and the difficulties he encounters by the lack of a distinction between denotation and connotation.

2. Metz implies that the nature of structural analysis is such that the shifting point of view is a methodological requirement accounting for the dynamic interaction of the elements found in structures.

An example of this appears in *Film Language* where he talks about the necessity of accepting, as a methodological

44

requirement, the principle of a "perpetual see-saw" (FL, pp. 143-144).

However, the "perpetual see-saw" is occurring between so many elements and simultaneously on so many planes and levels that confusion results. Coupled with the great obscurity of many of Metz's distinctions and the other shortcomings of his approach which are described in this chapter, the "perpetual see-saw" brings about a sense of disorientation.

An additional troublesome quality of this "see-sawing" is that Metz often describes in such a manner the activity occurring between structural elements that he gives the impression that he is talking about something which is alive. Of course, all the perceived activity is in the mind of the analyst, but Metz talks about this activity as if these elements within the structures were interacting with one another independently of the will and the consciousness of the analyst.

This practice cannot be dismissed merely as an element of the style of the author. Together with Metz's very frequent use of the term "object" in connection with things (such as "texts") which are not objects, this practice constitutes a deception. It is deceptive because it suggests that there is something tangible and verifiable about the structures and the activity occurring within them, when in reality we are not dealing with physical objects in the material world and therefore nothing really can be verified.

3. Metz utilizes a dialectical approach, or, at least, an approach freely inspired from dialectics, which advances on the basis of continuous and often overlapping transformations and polarities.

This aspect of Metz's approach permits him to do and to say anything he pleases, since he can assume any position he wants to assume and, at the same time, embrace the exact opposite position, or anything between these two extremes.

As a result of this constant shifting Metz becomes very elusive, and it is practically impossible to hold him accountable for anything. He covers all bases while occupying none.

4. Metz claims that his work is exploratory in nature and he is performing a task long overdue in the history of film theory. For this reason, he claims, it is proper for him to probe in different directions through successive questioning and not to be concerned with the fact that there may be inconsistencies in his approach.

Time after time in *Film Language* and in *Language and Cinema*, he expresses the hope that, somehow, the day will come when the problems he uncovers (or creates) will be solved through an increased efficiency of the cine-semiotic techniques.

This faith in the future is also expressed in "The Imaginary Signifier," but this time not in terms of linguistics but of psychoanalysis. In "The Imaginary Signifier," however, Metz apparently has began to suspect that this constant shifting and his fragmenting of every dimension and every element he touches upon may never come to an end. He speaks of a "perpetual possibility of a finer...structuration," and of the fact that "the analyst will never complete his exploration of it [he means the system of a film] and should not seek any 'end'" (IS, pp. 35-36).

Circles, Spirals, and Lyrical Passages

The difficult situation in which Metz puts himself is also reflected in the circularity of his thought and in his very frequent excursions into a very lyrical style of writing during moments when he ought to be very precise.

Some examples of this situation and of the problems it creates are the following:

In *Film Language,* Metz says that "The specific nature of film is defined by the presence of a *langue* tending toward art, within an art that tends toward language" (FL, p. 59).

The above definition, cryptic and spiraling as it is, may appear to make some sense until one reads, six pages later, that "it seems appropriate to look at cinema as a language without a system" (FL, p. 65), and then ten pages later that "The cinema is not a language system" (FL, p. 75).

47

His definition (on page 59) of the "specific nature of film" also becomes an invitation to a very tortuous journey because the concepts of language system *(langue)* and language *(langage)* are drawn by Metz through the territory of art. In this section Metz becomes involved in his impossible distinctions and the matter of the specific nature of film remains unresolved.

The largest in number and the most troublesome of Metz's circles and spirals occur in *Language and Cinema*. Important parts of *Language and Cinema* where there is a great concentration of very disturbing circularity are Chapter I ("Within the Cinema: The Filmic Fact"), Chapter II ("Within the Filmic Fact: The Cinema"), and Chapter III ("Film in an Absolute Sense").

In these three chapters the "filmic" and the "cinematic" are drawn apart, forced to intersect, overlap, and fuse into one another. After proceeding in this manner for forty-five pages, he says:

> There is, however, one trait--and one alone--that is shared by all those things called "cinematic," in the loose sense of the word: they are all phenomena which are immediately discoverable in films, phenomena which are "found" in films, which the investigator can "attest" in films, which have films as their place of manifestation.
>
> In addition to being dangerous, as we have said, it is somewhat paradoxical to call these phenomena cinematic, since another adjective exists which is so-to-speak ready-made to refer to them and which would appear to be naturally (or rather linguistically) predestined to the task: the adjective filmic. In fact, what is filmic, if not the sum of what appears in films? (LC, p. 46)

Then, Metz tries to excuse his circularity by claiming

that this is a feature which appears in other fields:

> The quite considerable extent of this zone of overlap should not
> be surprising, and the overlap itself is no anomaly to be "done
> away with." This phenomenon of contextual neutralization is not
> restricted to the domain of the cinema (or to the film!); its
> equivalent may be found in other semiotic studies, even in
> linguistics. (LC, p. 57)

Finally, Metz blames this circularity on the lack of

"rigor" in film research:

> We can understand, then that if the distinction between cinema
> and film is sometimes a source of difficulties, it is not because
> the two notions are inherently ill-defined, or that their opposi-
> tion is complex and ephemeral, but rather than habits of rigor
> are less well established in research on the cinema than in
> other disciplines. (LC, p. 57)

Other examples of Metz's circularity and the overall

obscurity present in his work are the following:

> Every code is a system, and every message is thus a text. But
> the inverse is not true, and certain systems are not codes but
> singular systems (despite their systemic nature, they involve a
> single text); and certain texts are not messages but singular
> texts: they constitute the single manifestation of a system, not
> one of the multiple manifestations of a code. (LC, p. 75)

> Just as all that is codical in texts is general, everything which
> is general in texts is codical. (LC, p. 154)

> . . . in this code, syntagmatics and paradigmatics constantly
> refer back and forth to one another and are, properly speaking,
> inseparable . . . A code is both a paradigmatic and a syntagmatic
> mechanism. (LC, p. 170)

> All that which is specifically filmic is filmic, but all that
> which is filmic is not specifically filmic. (LC, p. 40)

In Chapter X ("Specific/Non-Specific: Relativity of

the Classification Used"), after attempting another major

distinction which ends in a circularity from which he cannot

escape, Metz declares:

> The two circles are "concentric" (an approximate metaphor, which
> should not be taken too literally). (LC, p. 229)

49

The impossible situation in which Metz places himself, and the general confusion which results from this, forces him to become quite lyrical and "impressionistic" during crucial moments in the development of his ideas when the "specificity" he has talked about ought to be present. A good example of this lyrical quality in *Film Language* involves his treatment of the concept of the "current of significa- tion," which he borrows from Bela Balázs, and which he renames the "current of induction" (FL, pp. 46-47).

According to Metz, this "current" accounts for the connections which are made in the spectator's mind when two images are juxtaposed. It is the force which "refuses not to flow whenever two poles are brought sufficiently close together, and occasionally even when they are quite far apart" (FL, p. 47). Considering that Metz places great emphasis on the syntagmatic dimension, this mysterious and almost mystical circulating "current" is a very disturbing impressionistic element in his work.

Language and Cinema, which is supposed to be one of Metz's major contributions to the new "scientific" litera- ture of the cinema, contains many lyrical elements. Here is a small sample of these lyrical elements:

1. Metz indicates that "each film is built upon the destruction of its own codes" (LC, p. 102).

How can a film "destroy" its own codes? Since he states very often that the codes are creations of the analyst, is this "destruction" performed by him? How?

Under what circumstances? For what purpose?

2. Metz describes activities between the film codes in
terms of harmony and peacefulness and then he adds:

> The system of the text is the process which displaces codes,
> contaminating some by means of others, meanwhile replacing one
> by another, and finally--as a temporarily "arrested" result of
> this general displacement--placing each code in a particular
> position in regard to the overall structure, a displacement
> which is itself destined to be displaced by another text. (LC,
> p. 103)

How does a system "displace" codes? Is there a

process of "contamination?" What does it consist of?

"Destined" to be replaced" What force determines this

"destiny?"

3. In his attempt to give examples and refer to actual

films that supposedly illustrate a point he is trying to

make, a rare occurrence in his writings, Metz talks in terms

of "luminocity," "existential fracture," "phenomenological

schizophrenia," "perceptual sequential derailments,"

"tragicomic sense of a constant and derisive reversibility

of possibilities," "aggressive-arbitrary variegation of the

image," "abundant, egotistical, playful exuberance of the

picture track," and "tortured cult of the female idol" (LC,

p. 113).

4. Describing the alleged activity between textual

systems in a film Metz points out that:

> . . . the plurality of textual systems in a film can never be
> resolved into a neutral co-habitation of this sort, for each of
> them is obliged to lay claim to the textual territory in its
> totality, such that this totality is perpetually torn apart by
> its opposing irredentisms. (LC, p. 120)

For some reason Metz makes a number of references in
his works to "irredentism" and the "irredencent" quality of
cinematic elements. He has never explained what is the
exact nature of this "irredentism."

Proof Via Manifesto and the Great Fear in the Horizon

Obviously Metz has a good understanding of the fields
of linguistics, structuralism, and psychology. Most of the
references to the methodological tools he borrows from these
fields are supported by invoking recognized authorities in
these fields. There is no doubt that he is well-versed in
film theory and, as indicated earlier, his awareness of the
reality of film is evident in all his writings.

Under these circumstances one would expect him to be
able to document the claims he makes about the manner in
which signification is achieved in motion pictures. This,
however, does not occur in his works. Metz always advances
from point to point via manifesto. Things are what he says
they are because he says so. He provides no evidence that
his conclusions are based on testing of any kind. Examples
in terms of actual films are very rarely given. When
examples are given they fail to add anything of real
significance to our understanding of the specific films
involved, or to our understanding of how films communicate.

His authoritanism and the lack of real scientific rigor
on his part are somewhat concealed by the fact that he is

almost constantly inviting the reader to go along with what
he is proposing for the sake of whatever argument he is
presenting. The impression is given that the reader is
invited to participate in an intellectual game which requires
agreement with statements which are extremely vague, circu-
lar, and unsupported by documentation and evidence.

In *Film Language* he devotes three out of his ten chapters to analysis of specific films in terms of his theoretical points. Chapters Six and Seven are an attempt to
analyze certain segments of Jacques Rozier's film *Adieu
Philippine*. Chapter Ten discusses the "mirror construction"
of Fellini's *8½*. In the remaining seven chapters there are
very few references to actual films and these references
are not related to any of the major points which Metz is
trying to make. Some hypothetical film scenes which Metz
creates and attempts to use as illustrations are too sketchy
and of little value to him and to the reader.

His "analysis" of *Adieu Philippine* is not really an
analysis but a process of choosing certain shots and scenes
from the film and affixing to them labels taken from his
incomplete classification system of the *Grande Syntagmatique*.
For example, he points to a series of shots of a boat which
are photographed and edited so as to capture the exhilara-
tion of sailing, and he informs us that this constitutes a
"descriptive syntagma" (FL, p. 173). Beyond this act of
labelling segments of *Adieu Philippine* there is nothing in

what Metz says which in any way indicates how this film communicates its ideas to us.

In Chapter Nine, a 7-page section hardly qualifying as a "chapter" in a book of over 250 pages, there is nothing in what Metz says about Fellini's *8½* which in any way supports the theoretical points made in the rest of the text of *Film Language*. In fact, this section is nothing more than a long digression from the main task at hand and it is related to cine-semiotics only in a very indirect and vague manner.

Metz's inability to provide evidence to support his claims is particularly disturbing in *Language and Cinema*. The very few attempts which are made in this book to relate to actual films what he is talking about are very disappointing. For example, his discussion of Griffith's *Intolerance* does not illuminate in any significant way his theoretical points. Certainly, Metz's semiotics does not seem to add anything new to our understanding of *Intolerance* through comments such as these:

> The cinematic technique of the film founded on parallelism quite .
> obviously shapes the notion of intolerance, such that in the end
> it becomes disengaged from the text, and floats toward a timeless
> horizon. (LC, p. 111)

In "The Imaginary Signifier," where the analyst and the analysand fuse into one and Metz ends up psychoanalyzing himself, the proof via manifesto technique is given a cloak of respectability by an outpouring of psychoanalytic jargon and the frequent invocation of the names of Sigmund Freud, Jacques Lacan, and Melanie Klein.

The fact that Metz appears to be operating under a great deal of stress has been mentioned already. What needs to be pointed out here is what I believe to be his greatest source of apprehension which always looms in the horizon: the reality of film.

Metz does not identify this source of fear as the reality of film. He talks only in terms of "culture." However, both his description of what is contained in "culture" and the context in which he uses the term indicate that he is referring to what I have called the reality of film.

In *Film Language* this fear surfaces a number of times. The most obvious manifestation of it occurs in his attempt to determine what is the minimum unit of signification in film. After preparing the reader for this observation by a number of references to what lies beyond the film, he says:

> Thus, when it reaches the level of the "small" elements, the semiology of the cinema encounters its limits, and its competence is no longer certain. Whether one has desired it or not, one suddenly finds oneself referred to the myriad winds of culture, the confused murmurings of a thousand other utterances: the symbolism of the human body, the language of objects, the system of colors . . . or the voices of chiaroscuro . . . the sense of clothing and dress, the eloquence of landscape. (FL, 142)

In Chapter Nine, he returns to the matter of the minimal units of signification which in *Film Language* he saw containing the "myriad winds of culture." After declaring that the shot is not the minimal unit, he argues that the identification of minimal units is not a "prerequisite for the entire domain of cinematic semiotics" (LC, p. 193). A few pages later he attempts to shut the door to the myriad winds of culture which the shot would usher in by stating that "the minimal unit is not a given in a text; it is a tool of analysis. There are many types of minimal units as there are types of analysis" (LC, p. 194).

Although in *Film Language* and in *Language and Cinema* Metz does not consider the content of films and he deals only with structural elements, in "The Imaginary Signifier" he seems to open the door which the image of the film represents. Standing at the threshold and confronting Metz are the myriad winds of culture and the sciences which study them: sociology, anthropology, history, etc. However, as we shall see in Chapter V, the opening of the door is deceptive. Metz is simply unable or unwilling to face the reality of film no matter what approach he takes in his study of how films communicate.

FOOTNOTES

[1]There are frequent references in Metz's works to the inadequacy of the conventional approaches to film theory and criticism. In *Film Language* see particularly the third chapter: "The Cinema: Language or Language System?" (FL, pp. 31-91). In *Language and Cinema* see pages 9-15, and pages 26, 34, 81-83, 115, 124, 266-267, 271-273. In "The Imaginary Signifier," see pages 21-25, 32-37, 39-40.

[2]See the works of Alan Lovell, Peter Wollen, Sam Rohdie, Geoffrey Nowell-Smith, and James Roy MacBean cited in the Bibliography.

[3]Saussure said in 1906 that "a science that studies the life of signs within society is conceivable . . . I shall call it *semiology* . . . since the science does not yet exist, no one can say what it would be; but it has a right to existence, a place staked out in advance." See Ferdinand de Saussure, *Course in General Linguistics* (London: Peter Owen, 1960), p. 16.

[4]*Film Language*, p. 91.

[5]For an analysis of the serious shortcomings of Metz's *Grande Syntagmatique*, see Jack Daniel, "Metz's Grande Syntagmatique: Summary and Critique," *Film Form*, 1, No. 1 (Spring, 1976), 78-90.

[6]For a good analysis of Metz's work see Brian Henderson, "Metz: 'Essais I' and Film Theory," pp. 12-33.

[7]The "filmophanic film" is, according to Metz, the film as experienced by the spectator during projection.

CHAPTER II

FROM MOVIES TO "CINE-TEXT"

The purpose of Metz's semiology is to create a model
which will enable him to explain how a film embodies meaning
and how this meaning is transmitted, signified, to an
audience.

According to the approach taken by Metz, the raw
material of the cinema out of which meaning arises is not
reality itself. The raw material is the various channels
of information which make up a film: image, graphics,
speech, music, and sound effects.

But even this raw material is not of interest to Metz.
His semiology is concerned with the logical structures
which operate on this material and which account for the
meaning transmitted to an audience.

A major problem with Metz's work is that, apparently,
he has not been able to decide exactly what is the nature
of the "film" which he makes the subject of his study. As
indicated in the previous chapter, in *Language and Cinema*
Metz claims that he is studying the "filmophanic film" as
perceived by the audience for the duration of its projection.

58

The problem is that the film as a signifying discourse (text), or as a linguistic object, and the filmophanic film perceived by an audience during projection are *not* the same thing.

Although Metz is well aware of the reality of film and he identifies correctly the channels of information which make up a film, in creating his analytic tools he does not deal with the filmophanic film. Everything he has to say about the semiotics of film in Film Language and in Language and Cinema is related to film as a linguistic object.

In "The Imaginary Signifier" Metz treats film as a dream and he attempts to study it with the tools of a vaguely described linguistic and psychoanalytic "inspiration."

The purpose of this chapter is to point out that in *Film Language* and *Language and Cinema* Metz regards films as "cine-texts," and he proposes analytic tools which prevent us from achieving contact with the reality of film.

This "reduction" of films to "cine-texts" is brought about by the banishment of the author,[1] by failing to take into consideration the content of films, and by dealing only with codes, sub-codes, structures, and systems which exist only in Metz's mind as analytic tools of his own creation unrelated to the reality of film.

According to the concept of the reality of film utilized in this study, the author of a film is the director who bases his work on the inspiration provided by the screenplay.

The matter of film "authorship" is a fairly complicated and controversial one. Something needs to be said about it here before comments can be made about Metz's problems with the banishment of the author in his works.

The concept of the director as the "author" of a film is European (basically French) in origin. This concept has become almost hopelessly entangled with the so-called "auteur theory" which is not a theory but, at best, a "policy of authors" attributed to some directors by certain critics.

This "theory" has not found wide acceptance in the United States and the title of "author" has not been applied to American directors by the majority of American critics because of the realities of film production in the United States. With a few, very few, exceptions such as that of an Orson Welles directing *Citizen Kane*, American directors working in this country did not have and continue not to have an opportunity to assume the full measure of control over the creation of their films to qualify as "authors."

When European critics accord the title of "author" (*auteur*) to certain American directors, they are doing so apparently without concern over the fairness of singling out these directors for such an honor while denying it to others.

Judging from the various lists of "author"-directors published in European film journals, it seems that the criterion used in granting the title of "author" to a director is that of liking his work. To be called an "author" is almost equivalent to being regarded as a "genius" by an admiring critic.

However, regardless of the measure of control which a director has over the creation of a film, the fact is that the director of a narrative film, at the very least, is the leader of the film crew and the coordinator of the activities of the creative people who make a film.

Actually, in most cases even in the United States, the director contributes enough to the making of the film to qualify as the person with the greatest amount of responsibility for interpreting the screenplay and making a film based on it. So it is relatively safe to say that the director is the "author" of a narrative film even if one does not give to the term "author" the meaning given to it by the European writers on cinema.

The screenplay, of course, is the blueprint for the making of a feature-length narrative film. One could hardly name a film of this kind which was not based on a screenplay, or, at least, on some kind of written outline.

The screenplay indicates the specific shots in which the plot is advanced, as well as the characters appearing in the film and the lines they speak. The screenplay also contains numerous pieces of information which indicate how the filmmaker should guide the audience's thoughts and feelings.

Taking all this into consideration, it seems that the study of how films communicate cannot exclude consideration for the screenplay and the director who interprets this screenplay in making a film.

Film theory and criticism of the conventional, non-structuralist persuasion has always dealt with the filmo-phanic film, and in doing so has always taken into consideration the director and the screenplay.

Although he claims that he is considering the filmophanic film, Metz disregards both the screenplay and the director.

This is so despite the fact that in *Film Language* there are a number of references to film directors and, as already indicated, despite the fact that he attempts to analyze one film (*Adieu Philippine*), and make some comments about another (Fellini's *8½*). In both of these cases Metz makes no comments about the director and the script which in any way illuminate his cine-semiotics. Also, he makes no comments in terms of cine-semiotics which illuminated either the director's work or the role which the screenplay plays in our understanding of how these two films communicate.

In *Language and Cinema*, a few references are made to film
directors. However, none of these references are related
in any vital way to the development of Metz's theories
about the codes or the other linguistic aspects of his
analysis. The same applies to consideration for the screenplay as the blueprint for the making of a film. Meaningful
references to the screenplay are missing even from the last
part of *Language and Cinema* which deals with "cinematic
writing."

In eliminating the author from the scene Metz is going
along with the theory of authorial irrelevance which has
been considered beneficial to literary criticism because it
shifts the focus of attention away from the author and
toward something more tangible--the work itself.[2]

With the author of the film out of the way, Metz
makes an effort to convince us that the "filmic text" is
somehow a real object which has qualities which the analyst
can discover and study. This is something which Metz
claims throughout *Film Language* and *Language and Cinema*.

However, in his attempt to be "scientific," Metz does
not merely eliminate the author. He eliminates the content
of a film in terms of theme, plot, characters, philosophical
underpinnings, and social commentary. In *Film Language* and in
Language and Cinema Metz refuses to consider any of the above
elements of the content of films.

In *Film Language* a key element in this banishment of the

63

content of films was his decision not to deal with the
"myriad winds of culture" which the image represents.

With the author and the content of films eliminated,
what is left for Metz to study? The answer is that he
invents something which he claims will help us understand
how films communicate, and then he proceeds to study *it*--
a product of his mind and not anything related to the
reality of film.

The procedure of inventing the object of his study is
introduced in *Film Language* and perfected in *Language and Cinema*.

In *Film Language,* after talking in a condescending manner
about previous efforts in the history of film scholarship
to deal with what he calls the "natural object" (the film in
terms of the reality of film), he announces:

> The grand moment, which one has been waiting for and thinking
> about since the beginning, is the syntagmatic moment. One
> reassembles a duplicate of the original object, a duplicate
> which is perfectly grasped by the mind, since it is a pure
> product of the mind. It is the intelligibility of the object
> that is itself made into an object.
>
> *And one never takes into account that the natural object has
> been used as a model. On the contrary, the assembled object
> is taken as the model object--and let the natural object
> keep still!* (FL, p. 36)[3]

Least we did not appreciate the difference between the
natural object and the reconstructed duplicate of it in the
mind of the analyst, Metz continues:

> The goal of the reconstruction, as Roland Barthes emphasizes,
> is not to reproduce reality: the reconstruction is not a
> reproduction, it does not attempt to imitate the concrete aspect
> of the original object; it is neither *poiesis* nor *pseudo-physis,*
> but a simulation, a product of *techne.* That is to say: the
> result of a manipulation. As the structural skeleton of the

64

object made into a second object, it remains a kind of
prosthesis. (FL, p. 36)

Operating under the impression that the natural object
can be silenced, Metz devotes the rest of *Film Language* to
dealing with the product of his *techne* by inventing for it
a "content" which he can manipulate and study.

In order to invent this content, and in an effort to
locate it somewhere, Metz attempts to make certain distinctions. As already indicated, he attempts to distinguish
between denotation and connotation. He also attempts to
distinguish between the syntagmatic and paradigmatic
dimensions. Both of these efforts, as already indicated,
eventually fail because of the circularity involved and
because of his inability to overcome this circularity.

But while denotation and connotation, as well as the
syntagmatic and paradigmatic dimensions, are being kept
distinct artificially for the sake of the argument he
presents, Metz weaves through these dimensions the concept
of *diegesis*. Since he is using a term/concept which in
ancient Greek thought has an established meaning which he
cannot completely disregard, he is forced to admit that
diegesis means "narration." Then, he admits that the term
was introduced to the field of cinema by Etienne Souriau
and that it designates

. . . the sum of film's denotation: the narration itself, but
also the fictional space and time dimensions implied in and by
the narrative, and consequently the characters, the landscapes,
the events, and other narrative elements, in so far as they
are considered in their denoted aspect. (FL, p. 98)

Then, Metz proceeds to use the concept of *diegesis* in connection with the product of his *techne* which has a content which is unrelated to narration, characters, landscapes, events, or anything else even remotely related to such elements. What Metz's *diegesis* is called upon to deal with are the structural relationships of elements which he calls the "syntagmatic components of films" (FL, p. 121) and which he describes in his *Grande Syntagmatique*.

In other words, Metz's *diegesis* does not refer to anything related to the reality of film. His *diegesis* is also a product of his *techne*. It is the organizing dimension accounting for a content which consists of the relationships between elements contained in the mental duplicate of the natural object! [4]

In *Language and Cinema* the journey into the phantom world of the cine-text is made in terms of elements of "narrativity" which Metz calls "cinematic language system," "code," "sub-code," "system," "message," "text," and "textual system."

A detailed examination of these elements inevitably will lead us to an analysis of Metz's work in terms of its place in the field of linguistics. Of course, this is not the purpose of this study. For this reason, only the abstract quality of these concepts and the manner in which they lead us away from the reality of film will be discussed here. Since Metz's thought is plagued by great circularity, a considerable amount of overlapping will be noted between these elements.

Before dealing with these elements it is appropriate to return to the role of the cine-semiotician as Metz sees it. In the beginning of *Language and Cinema*, he claims that:

> A semiotic analysis is thus closely associated with the aesthetics of film. (LC, p. 17)

However, nothing that Metz does in *Language and Cinema* is related to the aesthetics of film as we know the aesthetics of film. As was the case with his claim that he is studying the filmophanic film when he is not, Metz again indicates that he will do one thing and then proceeds to do something else.

This something else follows the pattern of what he discussed in *Film Language*. It is an examination of the duplicate of the natural object which (duplicate) is "perfectly" grasped in Metz's mind. In *Language and Cinema* the role of the semiotician is seen as follows:

> The semiotician follows a path which leads in the opposite direction from that of the cineast. The cineast starts with diverse . . . systems in order to arrive at a demonstrable text. The semiotician focuses on the text in order to reconstitute (and always explicitly) the systems which are implied by it, which are invisible in it, and which are discoverable in it alone. What the cineast constructs is the text, while the analyst constructs the system. (LC, p. 74)

Halfway through *Language and Cinema* he says:

> We would thus summarize the tasks of the semiotics of the filmic fact as follows: to analyze film texts in order to discover either textual systems, cinematic codes, or sub-codes. (LC, p. 150)

A few pages later he admits that the search for these

67

elements in the filmic fact is not related to the reality of film:

> At any particular moment, the analysis has nothing specifically to do with the film: behind it, in any case, are found only "films," and after it, thanks to it, "the film" begins to exist; not as a fourth term, but as part of the third (codes). When one claims to "study the film," what is meant is that, in a movement of reflection oriented toward cinematic codes and sub-codes, one forces oneself to organize a certain number of traits (which are themselves more or less general, and lacking a separate existence outside of the semiotic discourse) which present, in addition, the remarkable peculiarity of rejecting any immediate attribution to the code itself. (LC, p. 157)

Why this kind of analysis has nothing specifically to do with the film hopefully becomes apparent as we examine the elements of analysis which Metz brings to his enterprise.

Cinematic Language System

As Metz indicates in the Conclusion to *Language and Cinema,* the two great tasks involved in the study of the cinema is the analysis of the cinematic language system and the analysis of what he calls "cinematic writing" (LC, p. 286). The task of *Language and Cinema* is, essentially, to study the cinematic language system which he defines as "the combination of all the particular and general cinematic codes . . ." (LC, p. 69).

After Metz has an opportunity to reveal certain features of the codes, he returns for a refinement of his definition of the system. It is at this point that, as mentioned in Chapter I, he becomes very lyrical and he talks of the system being a process of displacing, deforming, and contaminating codes within the text (LC, p. 103).

The interesting thing about this cinematic language system turns out to be that it does not exist yet! The reason for this is that Metz does not produce the codes which must be contained in this system.

In the Conclusion to *Language and Cinema*, after he has spent approximately two hundred (200) pages describing in minute detail the intricate choreography of the activities of these codes, he states:

> . . . the reader will perhaps be surprised at not having found here an explicit enumeration of specific codes. This omission was intentional. First, because to study the status of a phenomenon (to define it intentionally) and to deploy its entire content (to define it extentionally) are two distinct steps and that, when the "phenomenon" is rather a constructed notion (as is the case for the cinematic language system), the detailed exposition of distinctiveness is what should take pride of place. Next, because cinematic studies are not yet developed enough; one is not able to seriously advance an explicit list of all the codes and sub-codes. It is, of course, possible, even desirable, to proceed already to a preliminary listing, to propose a beginning of an enumeration, even if incomplete and still approximate. But even this is a task which, in order to be useful, demands specifications which would require a separate book. (LC, p. 286)

Cinematic Codes and Sub-Codes

Although he is not able to produce a list of codes and sub-codes, Metz seems to know a lot about their characteristics and their behavior. This is not very surprising when one considers Metz's definition for the code and sub-code, his explanation of how they come to exist, and the function which he claims they have in his cine-semiotics.

In defining what a "code" is, Metz returns one more

69

time to a description of the nature of semiotic analysis:

> The semiotic analysis does not create the film, which it finds
> already made by the cineast. On the other hand, we can say
> that, in a certain manner, the analysis "creates" the codes of
> the cinema; it should elucidate them, make them explicit,
> establish them as objects, while in nature they remain buried
> in films, which alone are objects which exist prior to the
> analysis. It should, if not invent them, at least discover
> them (in the full sense of the term). It should "construct"
> them, which is in one sense to create them.
> ....
> The codes of the cinema are not things which one can immediately
> discern somewhere, for the cinematic does not exist independently;
> only an analysis can separate it out. It thus consists only of
> what the analyst puts in it. The analyst's task, in sum, is to
> uncover certain filmic facts and to construct the cinematic codes
> by means of these facts. (LC, p. 49)

Although Metz states repeatedly that the codes are

analytic tools which are the product of the analyst and they

do not directly express empirical reality (LC, pp. 54, 78,

79, 141, 154), the suggestion that these codes are created

by material provided by "certain cinematic facts" (LC,

p. 49) and by "materials furnished by the message" (LC,

p. 54), makes one hope that these codes, somehow, are

related to the reality of film.

However, nowhere in *Language and Cinema* does Metz explain

what "materials" the film offers to the analyst so that he

can devise from them the codes and sub-codes. Regardless of

the contacts with the reality of film that Metz alludes to,

his codes and sub-codes (which are codes appearing only in

certain types of films) remain very abstract notions which

exist only in the mind of the analyst.

Of course, this means that all of the activities of the

codes which Metz describes in endless detail are also in the mind of the analyst and not in the film.

This does not prevent Metz from often describing these activities as if they were occurring within the film independently of the consciousness of the analyst. For example, in talking about the "textual systems," Metz claims that

> It is not a question, then, at present, of examining individually each of the codes that the film contains in order to see if it is or is not of cinematic origin . . . What we are considering now are not the partial systems integrated by the film, but the activity of integration (or disintegration)--the process of composition or "writing"--by which the film, relying on all of these codes, modifies them, combines them, plays them one against the other, eventually arriving at its own individual system, its ultimate (or first?) principle of unification and intelligibility. (LC, p. 100)

Metz resorts so often to this anthropomorphism of the film, and he engages in so many practices which create the impression that we are dealing with something concrete and "real" when actually we are not, that one eventually comes to suspect that Metz is simply cheating.

The suggestion that Metz may be cheating has been made by at least one writer in connection with the concept of the code. Professor Gilbert Harman points out that Metz (and fellow semiologist Peter Wollen) cheats when he uses the term "code" interchangeably to mean "standard" or "cipher."[5]

The only hope raised by Metz that there can be some codes which are related to the reality of film comes in the form of what he calls "extra-cinematic codes." These are codes which appear in films as well as in other arts. They consist of what Metz calls "filmed-objects-of-a-fixed-psychoanalytic-value," and of "themes" such as those found in the Western.

In discussing briefly these "extra-cinematic" codes, Metz is forced to admit that they reflect society, culture, and human values. However, he shows very clearly that he has no intention of allowing these contacts with the reality of film to interfere with his work. He excludes these "extra-cinematic" codes from his study by associating them with the "filmic" and not with the "cinematic" which is the focus of his study. It should be remembered that Metz has not been able to make a clear and convincing distinction between the "filmic" and the "cinematic."

Metz justifies the exclusion of the "extra-cinematic" codes from his study out of fear of descending to the level of "cinematic journalism":

> As for the extra-cinematic codes, we have mentioned them only in order to recall that they play an important role in films. But a study of these codes could not be made the goal of the analyst of the cinema, nor of the analyst of films. Neither is it a question of a unified study, i.e., a "discipline." The extra-cinematic material found in films is as extensive and varied as social life itself (from which it directly stems), and its analysis relies upon quite diverse skills and a large number of pre-existing disciplines. In the division of labor customary today, one always has the tendency to confound the cinematic and the filmic, and to expect from the analyst of the cinema a science which covers all aspects of all films. It is not understood that this would be an almost universal undertaking, because films may be about anything. The immoderation of the expectation only encourages cinematic journalism. (LC, p. 150)

System

Another element in Metz's reduction of films into

72

linguistic objects is the concept of the "system." He says:

> Nevertheless, one should not forget . . . that what the analysis
> is trying to bring to light--and which is no longer a code--is
> still a system. The goal toward which all descriptive work
> strives is not the film as a real discourse (a series of images,
> sounds, and words arranged in a certain order, an object that
> may be attested) . . . What a description hopes to establish is,
> rather, the system which organizes this realization: the
> structure of the text, and not the text itself. The system is
> nowhere clearly visible in the actual unwinding of the film: a
> system, as such, is never directly attested. (LC, p. 73)

A few pages later he adds:

> What characterizes the systemic (the non-textual) is its nature
> as a residual object constructed by the analyst. The system has
> no physical existence; it is nothing more than a logic, a prin-
> ciple of coherence. It is the intelligibility of the text, that
> must be presupposed if the text is to be comprehensible. (LC,
> pp. 75-76)

With expressions such as "trying to bring to light,"
and "the intelligibility of the text that must be presup-
posed," Metz hints that the system may really exist in a
film and merely waits to be discovered by the analyst.
While hinting that the system may exist independently of the
analyst, he indicates that it is an analytic tool created by
the analyst. Then, when it suits him to do so, he comes
back to the idea that the system is real and merely awaits
to be brought to the surface by the analyst:

> It is characteristic of all cultural facts that they function
> according to systems but are not felt or experienced as such.
> It is distinctive of such systems that they remain unfixed,
> purely implicit, submerged in history as well as individual
> variations, etc.--but it is also distinctive that they appear
> more and more clearly as systems as our analysis of them
> gradually advances. (LC, p. 86)

At one point Metz attempts a distinction between a
system and a "singular system" and he gives the impression

that the "singular system" could be related to a certain dimension of the reality of film. However, he immediately takes steps to prevent this from happening. He says:

> However, we should be cautious about saying that singular systems are "real," for a system is never real (only a text is). If the singular systems seem to be real, it is because they are singular, and thus located in a unique and "concrete" place. But this place is concrete only to the extent that it is a text. The corresponding system, for its part, is nowhere made explicit, even in this place . . . Thus the system is not "real," which is why it is a system (a fabrication of the analyst-like codes). (LC, pp. 78-79)

Message and Text

"Message" and "text" are two more elements in the reduction of films to "cine-texts." In *Language and Cinema* Metz says:

> If the film--the message--is a "concrete" object, it is because its borders coincide with those of a discourse which has been effectively sustained, a unit which precedes the intervention of the analyst. (LC, p. 24)

However, Metz does not regard the "film" and the "message" as being one and the same thing. Later on he says that "message" is merely a part of a "terminological pair" (text/message) which stands opposite to the terminological pair of "system/code."

Then, he shifts his point of view and he talks in terms of the "message of the code" (LC, p. 75).

The matter becomes further complicated when he indicates that a "message" is actually the "text" of a "singular system." Then he shifts again his point of view and points out that

Films . . . are not messages but texts, for each of them contains several codes and many messages. (LC, p. 89)

Finally, he admits that:

Since a message is the text of a single system and since in a domain with a single semiotic dimension all texts are studied in relation to but one of their systems, message and text may in practice (and provisionally) become synonymous. (LC, p. 145)

Earlier, in *Language and Cinema*, he had indicated about the term "text" that:

It is evident that this term, for us, does not apply solely to the verbal element of the film . . . But we will take it here in Hjelmslev's sense, that is to name any semiotic expression . . . whether it is linguistic, non-linguistic, or a combination of both . . . A series of images is also a text, as is a symphony, a sequence of sound effects, or a series including images, sound effects, and music, etc., together. This point will be further discussed, in regard to the film, in Chapter 8.5. (LC, p. 87)

However, neither in Chapter 8.5, or anywhere else, does Metz deal with the concept of the "text" in a way which indicates that it contains any aspect of the reality of film such as the image or the soundtrack of films.

As for the term/concept "message," since he has used the term "film" in so many different ways ranging from the filmophanic film to a linguistic object, one becomes disoriented and does not know what Metz means by "message."

System/Code, Text/Message

The fact that Metz relates the concepts of system, code, text, and message has already been indicated. For the sake of appreciating the degree of abstraction which Metz utilizes and the distance from the reality of film from which he operates, I wish to quote him as he "plays" these concept/terms against one another. Compressing his text

75

to eliminate extraneous material emphasizes what the reader is confronted with as he tries to comprehend what Metz is saying:

Code always differs from message in that one is code and the other message. (LC, p. 59)

Thus the text, as text, is distinct from any system, and even from the unique system of which it is only text. And the system, even if unique, is distinct from any text, including its own. (LC, p. 73)

A code is a system which is valid for several texts (and these texts thus become messages); a message is a text which is not the only one to manifest a given system (and this system thus becomes a code). The system which is not a code (a singular system) has only one text; the text which is not a message (a singular text) is the only one to manifest its system. (LC, p. 76)

The problem of minimal units of signification in the cinema is reintroduced by Metz while he is discussing these concepts and the "play" which he fabricates for them.

In a move which seems to isolate his approach even further from the reality of film, Metz denies that there are minimal units of signification in the cinema which are not related to the code, and he denies that there is such a thing as a cinematic sign.

Concerning the minimal units he says:

No minimal unit (for specific systems of articulation) exists in the cinema; such a unit exists only in each cinematic code. (LC, p. 185)

The minimal units contained within the code have never been revealed by Metz. Therefore, his is a semiology which has never dealt with the problem of minimal units of signification.

The other unusual feature of Metz's semiology is that

he rejects the notion of a cinematic sign:

> There is no cinematic sign. This notion, like that of "pictorial signs," "musical signs," etc., stems from a naïve classification which proceeds according to material units (languages) and not by units of a logical order (codes). (LC, p. 194)

A few pages later, however, he feels the need to clarify the statement about the absence of cinematic signs and to separate this issue from his examination of the nature of the codes. He says:

> The notion of the sign . . . has no right to play a more important role in cinematic and filmic semiotics than in other areas of contemporary semiotics and linguistics. Without rejecting the notion of the sign as such, it must be realized that it only represents, today, one tool of research, and that it no longer enjoys the privileged and central status which it had with Saussure or Peirce . . . A system of signification is not only a system of signs; units larger or smaller than the sign play a considerable role in it. (LC, p. 207)

This reluctance to deal with the cinematic sign and the downgrading of its importance in the study of signification in the cinema seems to be important in terms of my concern for the reality of film. All of the approaches to the study of cinematic signs which I am aware of cannot help but deal with the image and through the image with the reality of film. Metz has no desire to deal with something which will involve the image and the reality it embodies. He prefers to deal with the abstract analytic tools of his *techne*. Metz admits this quite clearly when he summarizes what he has to say about the "specific/non-specific" aspects of his codes:

> In sum, the position which is adopted here includes two elements, not one: (1) the specificity which interests semiotics is the specificity of codes, not the "crude" specificity of physical signifiers; (2) the specificity of specific codes nevertheless refers to certain features of the material of expression. (LC, p. 219)

77

The crudity of the physical signifiers is rejected, but Metz never explains clearly what is the nature of those "features" of the material of expression. The material of expression, the image, graphics, speech, music, and sound effects, are merely identified and enumerated by Metz. He never deals with them in his work. As indicated a number of times, he is particularly reluctant to deal with the image.

So, the specificity of his codes remains a very vague notion. The vagueness of the concept of the code and the unreality of that to which Metz reduces movie films, the cine-text, becomes apparent when one tries to distinguish between his analytic tools and the object of analysis.

The object of analysis is an analytic tool, and the analytic tool is the object of analysis. Metz occupies most of his time analyzing his analytic tools and not film. The natural object, the movie film, has been forced by Metz to keep still.

FOOTNOTES

[1]This expression is borrowed from E. D. Hirsch who uses it in defending the view that a text means what its author meant it to say, or what a reader finds it to mean; what the linguistic signs themselves supposedly indicate that it means: See E. D. Hirsch, *Validity in Interpretation* (New Haven: Yale University Press, 1967).

[2]Hirsch, *Validity in Interpretation*, p. 2.

[3]My italics.

[4]For an interesting analysis of the shortcomings of the structuralist method and of that feature of structuralist criticism which transforms form into content, see Fredric Jameson, *The Prison-House of Language*.

[5]Gilbert Harman, "Semiotics and the Cinema: Metz and Wollen," *Quarterly Review of Film Studies*, 2, No. 1 (February, 1977), 15-24.

CHAPTER III

METZ AND THE FILM AUDIENCE

The purpose of this chapter is to look into the method
of analysis proposed by Metz in *Film Language* and *Language and
Cinema* in terms of those aspects of the reality of film which
involve the film audience. The material in this chapter is
divided in two parts: (1) Metz and the Limitations of the
Phenomenological-Structural Linguistic Methods, and
(2) Metz's Approach and the Film as Art.

Metz and the Limitations of the Phenomenological-Structural Linguistic Methods

In his attempt to isolate the "filmic object" so that
he can study it scientifically, Metz banishes not only the
author but the film audience as well. This banishment is
unavoidable. It is imposed by the phenomenological and
structural linguistic approach which Metz takes.

The phenomenological approach is nearly always purely
theoretical and requires a detached, contemplative, and
intuitive observation of the object of study. This object
is subjected to a "reduction" which consists of trying to
put aside all subjectivity on the part of the observer, all
hypotheses and proofs from other sources, and all tradition.

It seeks to isolate the "given object," the phenomenon.

Before the intellectual observation of the phenomenon can begin, the object must be further "reduced" by disregarding its existence and focusing on its essence.[1]

Phenomenological observation is analytical and descriptive. The analysis, an exegesis or hermeneutics, deals nearly always with structures because it is claimed that an important element of the essence of the phenomenon is its structure.

Phenomenology excludes most utilitarian considerations. The analyst contemplates the phenomenon for the purpose of attaining knowledge. The analyst's thought is focused exclusively on the object of his inquiry excluding everything that comes from himself in the form of attitudes, feelings, emotions, desires, and biases of all sorts. Of course, the objectivity of phenomenology is only an ideal.

The phenomenological aspects of Metz's approach create some serious problems as far as the role of the audience is concerned.

As we have seen, Metz disregards the natural object, the film, and he contemplates a pure product of his mind—"the intelligibility of the object that is itself made into an object" (FL, p. 36).

Although in the natural sciences the term "phenomenon" usually refers to something which can be observed directly through the senses (or indirectly through instruments), in phenomenology it is not necessary for the object to be observed in this manner. It is enough for the phenomenon to be imagined.

In Metz's writings, especially in *Language and Cinema,* the structural elements making up the phenomenon and the relationships between these elements are clearly imagined. Metz repeatedly admits that his codes, sub-codes, and the various systemic relationships are creations of the analyst and not properties of the object of his study.

An audience, however, is not relating to an abstract and imagined mental duplicate of the film. In a motion picture theatre the audience is experiencing very vividly through the senses of sight and hearing a "natural object" which is vibrating with a very strong impression of reality.

Accepting Metz's contention that his phenomenological relationship with the product of his *techne* explains how films communicate to an audience becomes a matter of faith and not scientific documentations. Metz and the film audience are relating to two different things.

Metz supposedly studies only what is "out there" without allowing his emotions to interfere with his efforts, and without incorporating anything in his analytic scheme which can account for the role of emotion in film communication.

On the other hand, the attitude of an audience cannot possibly be phenomenologically purged of emotions and feelings. An audience does not respond to a narrative film only intellectually. Emotions play a very important role in an audience's relationship with a film, and it does not seem possible to study how films communicate without taking into account the emotional aspects of an audience's response.

Phenomenology serves as the overall philosophical orientation of Metz's approach. The actual instrument of analysis is structural linguistics. It is the nature of this instrument that it excludes any consideration for the film audience.

A major conceptual tool of Saussurean linguistics is that of the sign and of the "internal" relationship between the signifier and the signified.

Focusing on the sign, this type of linguistic approach excludes any consideration for the object of reference in real life. Then, the signified is isolated and usually put aside. The analyst is then free to relate to the signifier and to formulate the syntagmatic and paradigmatic relationships which he sees as operating in connection with the signifiers.

Metz's work consists of theorizing about the nature of the signifier and of the functioning of the various analytic features which he invents for it. The relationship between the film audience and the signifier is not examined. Metz's analytic study takes into account only the relationship between the analyst and the signifier. As for the signified in film, it is excluded from consideration as a matter of principle. What is signified in film, to whom, in what manner, and under what circumstances is not examined.

Related to the concepts of the signifier and the signified are those of denotation and connotation. Structural linguistics places emphasis on denotation and so does Metz.

However, because of the nature of the film image, Metz is unable to distinguish between denotation and connotation. As we have seen, he admits that there is practically no way of keeping them apart in terms of the actual film-viewing experience. This does not prevent him from claiming that his interest lies in denotation and from proceeding to study what he considers to be denotation.

The denotation Metz deals with is not related to anything which is actually in the film. The denotation of his analysis turns out to be the relationships he creates for the analytic elements he invents for the mental duplicate of the natural object.

In this kind of scheme whatever Metz says about denotation in film is totally unrelated to what an audience comes in contact with as it views a motion picture.

As for connotation, it is not examined by Metz in terms of the analyst or the film audience.

Language changes over time and for this reason it is not a stable object of "scientific" analysis. The ingenuity of Saussurean linguistics lies in that it distinguishes between the synchronic and the diachronic dimensions of language and then focuses its attention on the synchronic. This solution is considered a "breakthrough" in the study of language because it allows language to be studied in a "static" state which, supposedly, yields valuable observations. At the same time the synchronic approach creates problems.

A very serious shortcoming of the synchronic approach is that the analytic methods it creates and utilizes may be appropriate (and the results they produce may be meaningful) for a given state in whatever is being analyzed, but not for all stages in the development of the object of study.

Another serious shortcoming of the synchronic approach, at least as practiced in most fields, is that it may yield seemingly useful information about individual segments of the object of study, but not meaningful in terms of our understanding of the subject as a whole.

Also, most synchronic studies tend to fragment the object of study without attempting a synthesis. We are left contemplating heaps of fragments which add little or nothing to our understanding of the subject.

Metz's approach is synchronic. There is nothing in his method of analysis which accounts for the fact that films consist of expressive elements which are presented to an audience and experienced by that audience diachronically.

There is nothing in any specific analytic procedure,

or in his overall method, which identifies the point in the history of the narrative film to which his approach is applicable. He allows us to think that his synchronic approach is valid for all periods in the development of the narrative film.

In interviews and while defending his work, Metz has made a number of admissions which indicate that his *Grande Syntagmatique* is an appropriate analytic tool only for a specific period in the history of motion pictures. He has indicated that this period may be that of from 1933/35 until about 1955.[2]

As far as *Language and Cinema* is concerned, he has never indicated that the procedures he describes in it are valid only for a specific point in the development of the narrative film. We must assume that these analytic procedures are valid for all periods in the history of film. However, since the role of the audience is completely eliminated in his approach, it is practically impossible to verify that his procedures are indeed applicable to all periods in the development of the narrative film.

The diachronic approach, which could have taken into account the role of the spectator in the development of the narrative patterns of film, is rejected by Metz because through such an approach "filmic orderings are codified primarily for purposes of connotation rather than denotation" (FL, p. 118). As we have seen, he is not interested

86

in studying connotation.

The limitations of the structural linguistic approach which Metz assumes also become evident in his refusal to deal with the audience in terms of the systems through which an audience maintains a contact with the reality of film.

In *Language and Cinema*, Metz identifies the main types of systems through which the audience experiences the total message of a film. These systems are an elaboration of the systems he mentions in *Film Language*. They are:

1. Visual and auditory perception.
2. The capacity of the audience to recognize, identify, and enumerate the visual and auditory objects which appear in film.
3. The ensemble of symbolisms and connotations which are associated with objects or relations between objects within the film.
4. The ensemble of principle narrative structures of a given civilization which are present in a film.
5. The ensemble of properly cinematic systems which organize the discourse of the elements presented to the audience by means of the preceding four elements. (LC, pp. 33-34)

Metz admits that elements (1) through (4) are cultur= ally acquired or influenced. Element (5) involves an organization of elements (1) through (4). In this fashion the dimension of cultural influence is very important in this organization of elements (1) through (4).

Since *Language and Cinema* supposedly represents Metz's major contribution to the development of the semiotics of film, one expects him to deal with the above systems. However, this does not occur. He simply fails to deal with elements (1) through (4). *Language and Cinema* attempts to

87

deal only with element (5), without any reference to the natural object, cultural influence, or the audience. The systems he describes in *Language and Cinema* are clearly identified as creations of the analyst, and they function according to rules borrowed from structural linguistic analysis. These systems merely describe how the analyst relates to the linguistic object/phenomenon.

In Metz's work there are frequent references to signification. In structural linguistics signification is viewed as a process. It is the act of the signifier and the signified combining to produce the sign. This process is not studied in order to discover what sort of meaning is conveyed through the act of semiosis. The object of the study is to determine how the union of the signifier with the signified produces meaning.

However, the problem is that structural linguistics has not provided us with a clear explanation of how semiosis is actually achieved. Exactly what occurs during the fusion of the signifier and the signified has never been deter-mined. Fredric Jameson points out that

> The emphasis on signification takes the form of a mystery, the mystery of the incarnation of meaning in language, and as such its study is a kind of meditation. This is what accounts for the hermetic quality of the writers who deal with it. The sense of the esoteric may be understood, in Barthes' sense, precisely as a sign, as a way of signifying ritual and the presence of mystery, of understanding through the very temporal unfolding of the ritual language the sacred quality of the object itself.[3]

To the basic inability of structural linguistics to explain exactly how signification is achieved, Metz adds the problems created by the fact that he does not take into account the signified. He is trying to demonstrate a process of signification which involves only the signifier.

In general terms, according to this scheme, the following factors are involved in signification:

1. In the cinema the material of expression out of which meaning arises is not reality itself but the channels of information: images, graphic elements, recorded speech, music, and sound effects.

2. Signification is the process of conveying messages to the audience through codes.

3. Codes are the logical relationships, the rules, which make possible the messages conveyed to the audience. The codes organize the material of expression to generate the messages or the meaning of the film.

4. Codes exist in systems in texts. The text can be a single film or a number of films.

5. The orchestration of the codes in systems is what causes the codes to "release" their messages (meaning) to an audience.

In terms of the place of the audience in Metz's work, the following comments can be made about his views on signification: When Metz talks about signification, he does not refer to the transmission of a so-called eidetic meaning --what a sign means. To achieve this Metz would have to take into consideration the signified and connotation. He

is referring to a purely operational meaning of the sign
which consists of knowing how the sign can be used in a
film. This operational meaning depends on the codes which
are creations of the analyst. The organization of the codes
into systems is also the creation of the analyst.

In *Language and Cinema*, Metz admits that

> Each film has its own structure, which is an organized whole, a
> fabric in which everything fits together; in short, a system. But
> this system is valid for one film . . . To the extent that films
> are considered as unique totalities, each contains within itself
> a system which is as unique as the film itself. (LC, p. 63)

So, when Metz is talking about signification he is
actually referring to the unique manner in which the analyst
manipulates the analytic features which he has created for
the purpose of relating to a film.

The audience can come into all this only if it were to
assume the role of an analyst of Metz's persuasion and were
to perform on a film the abstract logical manipulations
suggested by Metz. It seems very doubtful that a human
being seated in a movie theatre and experiencing a narrative
film could be engaged in such an activity.

Instead of telling us how a film communicates meanings
to an audience, Metz's approach describes the "interior
monologue" of Metz communicating with himself as he relates
to films. It is this procedure which he presents to us as a
new, revolutionary, and "scientific" theory which will
finally enable us to understand how films communicate.

Time after time in *Film Language* and in *Language and Cinema*,

Metz points out that his is a purely descriptive enterprise. There are no normative aspects to his work, he claims, and no attempt to evaluate what is being analyzed. This description, in typical structural-linguistic fashion, involves an infinite regression into dimensions which are progressively more and more abstract. Although Metz indicates that some day this descriptive enterprise will come to an end and a synthesis of sorts will take place, he does not want to predict when this synthesis will become possible or what form it will take.

Metz's claim that there are no evaluative and normative aspects to his work does not coincide with the facts. There are both normative and evaluative aspects, and he owes some of them to the nature of the structural-linguistic approach.

An important value judgment built into his work is the emphasis on the synchronic. Logically there is no valid reason why the synchronic approach yields more valuable information than the diachronic. Saussure's claim concerning the supremacy of the synchronic approach represents a value judgment on his part. Actually, the synchronic is merely another method of approaching and dissecting the object of study.

The emphasis on denotation at the expense of connotation can be viewed both as an evaluative and a normative feature of Metz's work which he owes to the structural linguistic method.

But the most prominent evaluative aspect of Metz's work

91

which he owes to structural linguistics and which is related to the role of the audience, seems to be what he calls the "principle of relevance" (LC, pp. 9-22, 71-73, 96-97, 122-124, 143-144). This is the principle which the analyst follows in making important decisions involving the materials of expression and the selection and manipulation of the analytic elements which the analyst creates. Since Metz claims that the work of the film viewer parallels that of the analyst, this appears to be a very important principle which lies at the heart of the question of how films communicate. Despite the apparent importance of this principle, Metz does not indicate what is its exact nature. He merely lets us know that it exists, and he moves on to other matters.

However, if the analyst can choose whatever he considers "relevant" according to a principle of relevance which has never been defined, so can the individual viewer of a film. In this manner Metz introduces a very disturbing impressionistic element which casts doubts about the validity of his claim that his is a scientific approach to film.

Metz's Approach and the Film As Art

Art is a social phenomenon. It is a process which involves the artist's experience of reality, the expression of this experience into an artistic medium, and the evocation of an experience in whose who come into contact with the work of art.

The audience's reaction to a work of art becomes part of the artist's experience of reality and it may influence the artist as he creates other works of art.

The audience's reaction to works of film art very much influences both the audience and the financial success of these works. Through its reaction to the produced and exhibited films the audience has exerted a tremendous influence in the choice of thematic material, the shaping of narrative patterns, the method of utilization of expressive means, and even the development of the technological aspects of film.

As it has been indicated already, Metz repeatedly admits in *Film Language* and in *Language and Cinema* that cinema is an art. But, when it comes to developing his analytic method which supposedly deals with how films communicate, he does not take into account that film is an art.

Also, Metz does not take into account that film is a social phenomenon. This comes about by completely disregarding the film artist (the "author"), by subjecting to analysis an abstract mental duplicate of the natural object (the film), and by substituting the analyst for the audience in dealing with the object of analysis.

What remains to be seen is whether or not the analyst deals with the mental duplicate of film in a way which accounts for the way an audience deals with the "real" film which is projected in a motion picture theatre.

Reflected in Metz's approach is a structuralist's
attachment to a cryptographic nature of reality which calls
for an emphasis on decoding and decipherement. Such an
approach requires that the analyst relates to the object of
analysis in terms of logic rather than emotions. The
phenomenological aspects of Metz's approach also call for a
relationship in terms of logic. As a result there is no
feature, aspect, or dimension of Metz's codes, sub-codes,
and systemic relationships which accounts for an emotional
involvement on the part of the analyst.

However, emotional involvement is a very important
feature of the relationship between an audience and a work
of art. In the narrative fiction film a great deal of the
information conveyed to an audience on the level of emotional involvement is through characters performing the
actions of the plot of the film. Consciously and uncon-
sciously a film is made so that the audience identifies with
one or more of the characters of the story. Metz makes no
effort whatsoever in *Film Language* and *Language and Cinema* to
account for audience identification as a factor in film
communication.

In the arts, especially the non-representational ones,
the question of subject matter is a very troublesome one
resulting in nearly endless and largely inconclusive debates.
In the art of film perhaps the situation is more clear
because much of what a film is about is expressed by the

plot and the events making up the plot. The representational quality of most images of most films also aids the audience in determining what a film is about.

Although Metz admits that "the event is still and always the basic unit of the narrative" (FL, p. 24), he completely ignores the event as an instrument of communication in the narrative film.

One reason for not being able to deal with the event, or with any other aspect of the plot, is his unwillingness to deal with the image which is inextricably bound with the subject matter of a film.

Metz's failure to deal with the image and with the events depicted through the image eliminates any consideration for important means of communication such as composition of the image, camera and/or subject movement, proxemic patterns, color, costumes, make-up, texture, lighting, sets, and the performance of actors.

Matters of tempo and rhythm within the shot and in the arrangement of shots into scenes and sequences, which is the source of great aesthetic pleasure and communication of important information to an audience, are completely eliminated by Metz's approach.

The fact that images often have metaphorical significance cannot be taken into account by Metz's methods because his semiological approach forces him to study only what he considers to be the denotative aspects of film.

In the art of film two very important expressive means at the disposal of the filmmaker are the manipulation of space and time. Narrative films tell a story from selected viewpoints which tend to fragment the dimension of space. While this is happening, the dimension of time can be expanded or contracted. This manipulation of space and time is a key element in controlling the flow of information to an audience and in determining the response of the audience to the film.

Despite his emphasis on the syntagmatic dimension of film and the structural relationships of the elements he sees operating in it, Metz fails to take into account the effect which the manipulation of space and time has on an audience. Again, the main reason why this occurs is that he refuses to deal with the image which contains a fragment of the time-space continuum.

Although he identifies the soundtrack as one of the main channels of information, there is nothing in his analytic tools which gives us even a clue as to how the various soundtrack elements communicate meanings to an audience.

The spoken word in the form of dialogue or narration which is the source of a great deal of information in narrative films is totally ignored by Metz. In view of his linguistic approach this is a very curious omission.

In *Film Language* and in *Language and Cinema*, there is no

analytic tool and no analytic procedure which accounts for
the manner in which music conveys to an audience extremely
valuable information on the intellectual and emotional
level. The same is true about the sound effects element of
the soundtrack. Metz merely identifies sound effects as one
of the elements of the channel of information which the
soundtrack represents. No attempt is made to examine how
information is communicated through sound effects.

Metaphorical uses of sound, which can be very rich
sources of information, are completely ignored by Metz.

The projection of a film in a motion picture theatre
constitutes a performance. It is, of course, a recorded
performance and as such quite different from one involving a
stage play. However, during the showing of a film there is
emotional interaction between the members of the audience
which is similar to the one that exists among members of an
audience experiencing a stage play. For an individual who
is viewing a film the experience is unique since in subsequent screenings of a film he is bound to react to it in a
different manner. This could be due to the fact that the
audience composition may be different, or because the
individual has already been exposed to the filmed performance
and he is communicating with it in a different manner.

In Metz's analytic procedures there is absolutely
nothing which accounts for the fact that in motion pictures
the spectator is a member of an audience witnessing a

performance.

Finally, Metz's analytic procedures fail to take into account the physical conditions under which the spectator comes in contact with a film and the psychological implications of these conditions. For example, Metz completely fails to take into account that the spectator is viewing a film in a darkened theatre and that his attention is focused on a two-dimensional picture within the boundary of a frame.

FOOTNOTES

[1] I. M. Bochenski, *The Methods of Contemporary Thought* (Dordrecht, Holland: D. Reidel Publishing Co., 1965), pp. 16-25.

[2] Daniel, "Metz's Grande Syntagmatique," p. 83.

[3] Jameson, *Prison-House of Language*, p. 169.

CHAPTER IV

THE SEVERED ROOTS

Narrative films are cultural objects within the social
process of communication.[1]

Making films, viewing films, and writing about films
are part of social interaction. As cultural objects films
reflect the ideas, beliefs, and values of the filmmaker. A
viewer relates to films in the context of his culture. The
film theoretician does not live in a social vacuum. He
approaches the study of films in terms of what is culturally
meaningful to him.

All of this represents an important aspect of the
reality of film and Metz is fully aware of it. However,
Metz's analytic procedures fail to take into account the
socio-cultural context of film.

The purpose of this chapter is to point out how Metz
indicates his awareness of the socio-cultural aspects of
film, and how his semiology operates in isolation from this
aspect of the reality of film.

Metz's awareness of the position which film occupies
within society and culture is demonstrated in *Film Language*
repeatedly. Some of the most obvious manifestations of this

100

awareness, other than the ones reflected in the extensive
quotes presented in the previous chapters, are the following:

> What we call "the cinema" is not only cinematographic language
> itself; it is also a thousand social and human significations
> that have been wrought elsewhere in culture but that occur also
> in films. (FL, p. 74)

> The merging of the cinema and of narrativity was a great fact,
> which was by no means predestined--nor was it strictly fortui-
> tous. It was a historical and social fact, a fact of civiliza-
> tion . . . a fact that in turn conditioned the later evolution
> of the film as a semiological reality. (FL, pp. 94-95)

In discussing problems of denotation in the fiction
film he distinguishes between two general types of signifying organizations: "cultural codes," and "specialized
codes" (FL, p. 112):

> The iconological, perceptual, and the other codes are cultural
> codes, and they function in good part within photographic and
> phonographic analogy. (FL, p. 113)

These codes are "natural" and they do not require that
the spectator be trained in any special way in order to
relate to them. It is sufficient for someone to be living
in, and to have been raised in, a given society.

On the other hand,

> The purely cinematographic signifying figures studied here
> (montage, camera movements, optical effects, "rhetoric of the
> screen," interaction of visual and auditory elements, and so on)
> constitute specialized codes . . . that function above and beyond
> photographic and phonographic analogy. (FL, p. 113)

He acknowledges that films contain "fragments of
reality" which reflect cultural significations.

> The mechanical character of the basic filmic operation (photo-
> graphic and phonographic duplication) has the consequence of
> integrating into the final product chunks of signification whose

101

internal structure remains afilmic, and which are governed mainly
by cultural paradigms. When some of these "fragments of reality"
have been specially produced for the film (i.e., *mise en scène),*
this production itself . . . is never entirely obedient to systems
that are unique to the art of film, but rather in large part to
those same cultural significations that intrude into the filming
of an object. (FL, pp. 139-140)

As it has been indicated in previous chapters, Metz

acknowledges that the competence of the semiotics of the

cinema eventually encounters its limits because in trying to

discover the smallest unit of cinematographic signification

one eventually becomes confronted with the "myriad winds of

culture" (FL, p. 142).

In putting forward his principle of the "see-saw,"

which operates between "the screen instance (which signi-

fies) and the diegetic instance (which is signified)," Metz

points out that

This see-sawing . . . is nothing other than the consequence of an
underlying cultural and social fact: The cinema, which could
have served a variety of uses, in fact is more often used to tell
stories. (FL, pp. 143-144)

Metz's discussion of certain theoretical problems

involving "the modern cinema and narrativity" gives him the

opportunity to make a comment which is significant in terms

of his failure to consider the sociocultural dimension of

film:

Remove "drama," and there is no fiction, no diegesis, and
therefore no film. (FL, p. 194)

While dealing with the work of Pier Paolo Pasolini,

Metz admits that:

. . . when very broadly cultural codifications occur in films--as
they do frequently, especially when one thinks of the contents of

102

individual films--they are often present in the image itself (or
in the sound itself)--that is to say, within the "analogy," or at
a point that, in relationship to the total economy of the filmic
signification, is distinct from that occupied by the codifications
that constitute what one calls "cinematographic language." (FL,
p. 215)

Then, he attempts to make a distinction which points again

to the sociocultural dimension of film:

The image of the wheels of the 'train derives from society, not
from the cinema; when it appears on the screen it is identified
by visual analogy with the real wheels of a train, and it is
thanks to this resemblance that the film is able to carry all
the additional significations associated with the image in
culture. (FL, p. 215).

Afraid, perhaps, to open the door to the "myriad winds of

culture," he quickly points out:

But if the image is ordered along with other images in an alternate montage . . . another kind of codification emerges, one that
is specifically cinematographic and is no longer broadly cultural,
and is superimposed over the visual analogy and not merged with
it. Similarly, one must point out that cultural codifications,
when they occur in films, often appear on the level of the actual
filmed "objects," whereas cinematographic codifications mainly
affect the disposition of the objects once they are filmed. (FL,
p. 215)

Forced once more by the inadequacy of his approach into

attempting another impossible distinction, Metz immediately

tries to find a way out of the difficult situation in which

he has placed himself. He says:

There remains, of course, a problem, and that is that cinematographic language itself, in as much as it is a body of orderings,
must certainly be influenced by various sociocultural codifications: Just as the "filmed object" retains the meaning it had
outside the film, the types of filmic orderings must in one way or
another refer to given patterns of intelligibility within society.
Thus, parallel montage is a peculiarly cinematographic figure, but
it is inconceivable that it could legitimately exist in the cinema
in a society that had no prior notation (in its language, its
writings, its "logic," etc.) of the symbolic and intelligible
value of certain very general types of relationships such as
alternation, parallelism, antithesis, etc. (FL, p. 215)

Metz admits that there are three types of influence,
"censorships" as he calls them, which determine the content
of narrative films: "censorship of moral standards"
(censorship proper), "economic censorship," and "ideological
censorship" (FL, pp. 236-237).

According to Metz, operating around, beside, beneath,
and larger than institutional censorship, there is the
"censorship of the Plausible," a "reduction of the possible,"
which determines the manner that film subjects are handled.
He claims that the Plausible is cultural and arbitrary and
varies according to the country, the period, and the genre
(FL, pp. 239-244).

Metz acknowledges that

> Since the film-maker shoots films, to some degree he often shoots
> the films of other people, believing that he is shooting his own.
> To tear oneself away, even partially, from an attraction so
> profoundly rooted in the fact of culture, in the shape of fields,
> requires unusual strength of mind. Books reflect each other, so
> do paintings, and so do films. (FL, p. 245)

In *Film Language,* Metz excludes the sociocultural dimension of film through the following:

He fails to examine the role which visual perception
plays in experiencing films. He does not formally take into
account the numerous studies which have been conducted on
visual perception, and he does not incorporate in his work a
study of his own. The very few observations he makes on how
audiences perceive films are unsupported by evidence and
they appear to be nothing more than his impressions of the
subject.

104

By not taking into consideration the mechanics of perception, he is unable to deal with what an audience brings to the viewing of films in the form of cultural conditioning, and he cannot explain how an audience relates to the aspects of culture contained in the images and sounds of a film. Considering that he claims to be very much concerned with the problem of the "impression of reality in films," his failure to deal with something as fundamental as perception constitutes a major weakness of *Film Language*.

It must be remembered, of course, that Metz does not deal with the natural object but with a mental duplicate of it which he has invented. He mentions visual perception a number of times, but the product of his *techne* is unrelated to visual perception.

After he states that there is a distinction between "cultural" and "specialized" codes, he abandons the cultural codes and attempts to examine signification in the cinema only in terms of the specialized codes.

However, he completely fails to indicate how the specialized codes function "above and beyond photographic and phonographic analogy." His subsequent comments about the "chunks of signification" which are governed by cultural paradigms and which are contained in the "final product," indicate that he is unable to make a clear distinction between the cultural and the specialized codes.

Although he is forced to admit that the "see-saw

principle" operating between the signifier and the signified is the consequence of the underlying cultural and social fact that the cinema has been used to tell stories, he fails to examine the cultural and social aspects of his "see-saw principle." The same thing occurs in connection with the dramatic-theatrical dimension of film. Metz *does* remove "drama" and all the sociocultural aspects associated with it.

Metz does not provide any element in his analytic procedures which can deal with the four kinds of cultural and institutional "censorships" which he sees operating in film and which determine the handling of film subjects.

Since he indicates that these "censorships" are very much related to the manner in which films signify, his failure to account for these "censorships" constitutes a major flaw of his analytic procedures.

He makes no effort whatsoever to determine how the culturally conditioned Plausible influences signification in the cinema.

In *Film Language* Metz does not suggest any method for dealing with the "fact of culture" that films reflect one another. However, this "reflection" is an important element in terms of signification, and his failure to take it into account is another major flaw of his analytic procedures.

Metz claims in *Film Language* that some of the central questions in the semiology of the cinema are successivity,

precession, temporal breaks, causality, adversative relationships, consequence, spatial proximity and distance (FL,
p. 98).

All of these matters are inextricably related to
perception and sociocultural conditioning. His *Grande Syntagmatique* supposedly represents a master plan accounting for
intelligibility in filmic discourse. However, the procedures which gave birth to the *Syntagmatique* and the master plan
itself ignore the sociocultural dimension of all the central
questions in the semiology of the cinema.

In *Language and Cinema* some of the ways by which Metz
indicates his awareness of the social context within which
cinematic signification occurs are the following:

Language and Cinema opens with the statement that the
cinema is a vast and complex sociocultural phenomenon and
an established cultural fact (LC, p. 9).

He distinguishes between the cinematic and the filmic
"fact" and points out that at the center of the cinematic
fact lie technological, economic, and sociological dimensions (LC, p. 12).

He admits that because film is a "closed text" like a
myth, a play, or a novel, it is a "total cultural object"
(LC, p. 18).

As has been indicated, Metz claims that the total
message of the film becomes comprehensible through five
types of systems: visual and auditory perception, recogni-
tion, identification, and enumeration of visual and auditory

107

objects, the ensemble of "symbolisms" and connotations which
are associated with the objects, the ensemble of narrative
structures which are present in a given civilization, and
the ensemble of properly cinematic systems (LC, pp. 33-34).

Metz points out that the first four of these systems
are cultural and acquired by living in a given culture. As
a result of this later on he is forced to admit that a film
is not only an example of cinema but also of culture (LC,
p. 72).

He declares that cinema is a "rich language system" and
identifies such a system as "one which is open to all
social, cultural, aesthetic, ideological, etc., influences
and initiations" (LC, p. 35). Also, he declares that "the
cinema is one of the language systems endowed with some
sociocultural depth" (LC, p. 36), and that

> The cinema . . . like all rich languages, is largely open to all
> symbolisms, collective representations, and ideologies, to the
> influence of diverse aesthetic theories, to the infinite play of
> influences and filiations between different arts and different
> schools, to all the individual initiatives of film-makers
> ("revivals"), etc. (LC, p. 37)

He admits the social status of film by saying that all
films are a work of art and that they function socially as
works of art (LC, p. 38). He emphasizes the social function
of the cinema by adding that

> . . . the cinema, like literature or the theatre, is in principle
> capable of saying anything, and conveys non-specialized signi-
> fieds which are above all ideological and cultural, and could be
> found just as well . . . in other language systems utilized by
> the same civilization during the same period. (LC, p. 39)

Metz knows that there is an ideological-political

dimension in films, and, for this reason, consciously or
not, films reflect systems of political thought (LC, p. 99).

The fact that films reflect social behavior is admitted
by Metz a number of times. He locates the reflection of
social behavior in the "extra-cinematic material" which, he
claims, is "as extensive and varied as social life itself
(from which it directly stems)" (LC, p. 150).

Some of the specific ways by which Metz fails to
consider the sociocultural dimension of film are the
following:

After he distinguishes between the "cinematic" and the
"filmic fact," he chooses to deal only with the "filmic";
rejecting the "cinematic" at whose center lie the technological, economic, and sociological dimensions of film. Then,
he declares that the "filmic fact" is still too vast and
unmanageable an area because the "filmic fact" contains
psychological, sociological, and aesthetic phenomena (LC,
p. 16). He proceeds to eliminate from consideration these
dimensions of the reality of film by dealing with the
"filmic fact" only as a "language system."

After he identifies the five systems through which
the total message of the film becomes comprehensible, he
puts aside the first four, which are acquired through
cultural conditioning, and he develops his analytic procedures around the fifth which he labels "properly cinematic."
This is very similar to his ignoring of the "cultural codes"

in *Film Language* and attempting to deal only with what he calls the "specialized codes."

He fails entirely to deal with film as an art form and with film aesthetics in terms of the traditional concerns of film aesthetics. As a result, he provides no feature in his analytic procedures for handling the social status of film as an art, and he does not concern himself at all with sociocultural aspects of film aesthetics.

He distinguishes between "cinematic" and "extra-cinematic material" and points out that the "extra-cinematic are the elements which reflect social life. Then he proceeds to examine only the "cinematic" and to leave out everything which reflects social behavior, ideology, and the important economic elements of the reality of film.

He does not examine the relationship between the codes of sight and the codes of spoken language although he acknowledges the existence of very close ties between the "visible world" and language. In this manner he fails to investigate the cultural dimensions of language and, through them, the cultural dimensions of visual perception as they relate to film.

Although he identifies cinema as a "rich language system," he fails to provide any feature in his analytic procedures which accounts for the social, cultural, aesthetic, and ideological influences to which such "rich" systems are susceptible.

He discusses extensively cinematic "systems," but he

views the concept of the system in the structuralist tradition and in a manner which hermetically seals out the sociocultural dimensions of film. He points out, characteristically, that

> What the word system implies, in all its uses, is that one is thinking of a coherent and integrated ensemble--an "autonomous entity of internal dependencies," as Hjelmslev said of the notion of structure--of an ensemble within which all the elements hold together and have a value only in relation to one another. (LC, p. 84)

He admits that the notions of code and sub-code do not directly express empirical reality but they are analytic tools which are creations of the analyst (LC, p. 141).

However, he shifts his position and makes the codes and sub-codes appear to be elements of the empirical reality which films represent. He says:

> The film must be lighted and must be edited. The cineast will necessarily choose, in either a conscious or intuitive manner, a sub-code of lighting and a sub-code of montage. (LC, p. 142)

Then, he continues:

> The plurality of the sub-codes is due to the fact that the solutions to these problems are in turn quite diverse: it is not exactly the composite of the "cinematic" that it reflects, but its historicity, its variations from one epoch to another, etc. The ideal sum of sub-codes . . . constitute nothing more than the history of the cinema, at least insofar as what is truly cinematic is concerned. (LC, p. 143)

In the paragraphs which follow he excludes the "extra-cinematic" from his approach, and in this manner he leaves out the sociocultural dimensions of film which the "extra-cinematic" represents. He says:

> As for the extra-cinematic codes, we have mentioned them only in order to recall that they play an important role in films. But a study of these codes could not be a goal of the analyst of the

111

cinema, nor of the analyst of films. Neither is it a question of
a unified study, i.e., a "discipline." The extra-cinematic
material found in films is as extensive and varied as social life
itself (from which it directly stems), and its analysis relies
upon quite diverse skills and a large number of pre-existing
disciplines. (LC, p. 150)

He makes no effort to examine the sociocultural aspects

of the "material of expression" of films although he points

out that

"The material of expression," as its name indicates, is the
(physical, sensorial) material nature of the signifier, or more
exactly of the "fabric" into which these signifiers are woven.
This fabric may be phonetic...aural but not phonetic...visual and
colored...visual but not colored...it may consist of movements of
the human body...etc. (LC, p. 208)

Although he observes correctly that meaning in film

communication is psycho-sociological in nature (LC, p. 211),

he fails entirely to deal with meaning in psycho-sociolog-

ical terms. Instead, he approaches the matter of meaning in

structuralist terms and identifies it with the relationships

of the various signifying elements operating within the

systems. ·

He labels "extra-cinematic," and thus he excludes from

consideration, important aspects of the reality of the

content of films such as:

. . . a given collective representation or some social *imago* (the
seductor, the model spouse, the wayward youth, the adventurer,
etc.) which appear in films as well as in books, newspapers, and
conversations, at least within a given cultural area. (LC,
p. 213)

In discussing the "specificity" of the cinematographic

codes, he points to the existence of "visual-iconic codes"

which are of great anthropological importance. He labels

these codes "codes of analogy" and he observes that they represent

> . . . a whole ensemble of psycho-physiological montages, inte-
> grated with the perceptual activity itself, and whose modalities
> vary noticeably from one culture to another. (LC, p. 228)

Then, he proceeds to minimize the importance of these "codes of analogy," and he eventually fails to take them into account in his examination of cinematic signification on the grounds that the "picture track" of the film is not sufficiently defined by its iconicity.

In *Film Language* and in *Language and Cinema,* Metz's failure to take into account the sociocultural dimension of film appears to stem from his aversion to anything which might be regarded as normative, and from his insistence on maintaining what he considers to be a purely descriptive and "scientific" approach to filmic signification. As he points out time after time, the audience "reads" a film in a "naïve" (cultural) manner, while the film semiotician reads it analytically and scientifically.

However, as the editors of *Cinethique* point out in terms of their own interest in marxist film theory, Metz's "neutrality" and his concept of scientific experimentation as independent of social practice is an illusion.[2] No matter what Metz says, it is unavoidable that a person in his position be subject to the same idealist determinations that govern the film viewer.

Metz's scientificity bears the external signs of

seriousness, rigor, method, and precision, but he fails to acknowledge that he is unavoidably dealing with film in terms of what is culturally meaningful to him. The result of pretending that he can remain "neutral" is that he fails to provide for any feature in his analytic procedures which can account for the semiotician's sociocultural viewpoint.

Under these circumstances, one wonders, in what setting, from what perspective, in terms of what time period reference, influenced by what set of values does the semiotician approach the study of film signification? Metz does not provide any answers to such questions. The consequences of failing to account for all of this is that Metz, who eliminates the author of the film, the concerns associated with film-making, and the manner in which an audience perceives the filmophanic film, has also eliminated, in essence, the film semiotician.

FOOTNOTES

[1] Andrew Tudor, *Image and Influence: Studies in the Sociology of Film* (London: Allen & Unwin, 1974), p. 137.

[2] *Cinéthique,* "On '*Langage et Cinéma*'" *Screen,* 14, No. 1/2 (Spring/Summer, 1973), 189-213.

CHAPTER V

THE IMAGINARY SIGNIFIER

In Chapter I there were a number of references to
Metz's psychoanalytic approach to film signification. The
purpose of Chapter V is to describe briefly the psychoanalytic approach which Metz establishes in "The Imaginary
Signifier," to relate this new direction to his earlier
structural-linguistic approach, and to point to the problems
that Metz encounters in terms of the reality of film.

This chapter is divided into three parts: "General
Characteristics and Features of Metz's Psychoanalytic
Approach," "From the Linguistic to the Linguistic-Psycho-
analytic Approach," and "The Linguistic-Psychoanalytic
Approach and the Reality of Film."

General Characteristics and Features
of Metz's Psychoanalytic Approach

The purpose of "The Imaginary Signifier" is, according
to Metz, to try to answer the question, "What contribution
can Freudian psychoanalysis make to the study of the cinematic signifier?" (IS, p. 28).

To achieve this he feels the need to first define what
he means by "contribution," "Freudian," and "cinematic

signifier."

Unlike the early days in his "intervention," when he proclaimed that the time had come for a semiotics of the cinema based solidly on semiotics, Metz is now much more cautious. He speaks in vague terms of a "psychoanalytic inspiration," and he admits that psychoanalysis cannot be the only discipline concerned with the study of the cinematic signifier. The "psychoanalytic inspiration" must be combined, he says, with "linguistic inspiration" because linguistics and psychology are two sciences both of which deal with signification (IS, p. 28).

However, both these sciences have to be set "within the horizon of a third perspective . . . the direct studies of societies, historical criticism, the examination of infrastructures" (IS, p. 28). This is so, Metz finally admits, because:

> In cinematic studies as in others, semiology (or semiologies) cannot replace the various disciplines that discuss the social fact itself (the source of all symbolism), with its laws that determine those of the symbolic without being identical with them: sociology, anthropology, history, political economy, demography, etc. (IS, p. 29)

Viewing now film from this expanded perspective, Metz comes to have a new hope:

> A combination of linguistic and psychoanalytic inspiration may lead gradually to a relatively autonomous science of cinema (=semiology of the cinema). (IS, p. 31)

As far as psychoanalysis is concerned, Metz points out that

> What I shall call psychoanalysis will be the tradition of Freud

and its still continuing developments, with original extensions such as those that revolve around the contributions of Melanie Klein in England and Jacques Lacan in France. (IS, p. 32)

The very crucial matter of defining that on which the linguistic-psychoanalytic inspiration will be applied, the "cinematic signifier," becomes the source of many problems for Metz.

Frankly, he admits, he is not sure yet what should be the overall orientation which will determine what aspect of film he will study. But he does know that he will not assume a "nosographic" approach. He defines this as an attempt to treat films as symptoms from which one finds access to the neuroses of the filmmaker, the script writer, etc. (IS, p. 32). Also, he knows that he does not want to engage in "psychoanalytically inspired characterology" (IS, p. 33). This is a version of the nosographic approach which places less emphasis on the pathological aspects of the filmmaker's personality.

What he finds wrong with these two approaches is that they are interested in persons and not the "discursive facts," which he defines as "filmic texts or cinematic codes" (IS, p. 34).

As a first and "somewhat simplifying step," he decides to call his approach "the psychoanalytic study of film scripts" (IS, p. 34). "Film script" is defined "broadly" as "the manifest thematic complex of the film," extending to a large number of features which may not appear in the written document commonly referred to as the screenplay, and which involves elements related to plot, situations, characters, "landscapes," "period details," etc. (IS, p. 34).

Defined in this manner, the "film script" is regarded by Metz as one aspect among others in the "textual system" of films. This "textual system," he claims, "shifts in the direction of the signifier" (IS, p. 36). Metz goes on to state that:

> To study the film script from a psychoanalytic (or more broadly semiotic) viewpoint is to constitute it into a signifier. In this the script is like a dream, as are many human products. The manifest dream, i.e., the dream as such--"dream content" for Freud...--is a signifier for the interpretation. (IS, p. 36)

Since there can be psychoanalytically oriented studies which treat the "film script" in terms of a signifier which is not "cinematic," Metz points out that his approach will consist of a "direct examination, outside any particular film, of the psychoanalytic implications of the cinematic" (IS, p. 41).

In linguistic terms, Metz claims

> . . . what calls for psychoanalytic illumination is not just each film (not just films) but also the pertinent features of the matter of the signifier in the cinema, and the specific codes that these features allow: the matter of the signifier and the form of the signifier, in Hjelmslev's sense. (IS, p. 42)

The aspects and features of the cinematic signifier which Metz claims need to be studied are the following:

1. Visual and auditory elements of the signifier since the signifier is perceptual in nature (IS, p. 46).

2. Fantasy aspects of the signifier since it consists of images appearing on a screen which is an "area" more

119

closely associated with fantasy than is the theatrical
stage.

3. "Fictive" aspects of the "unfolding" of the images
on the screen, in the sense that the actor, the decor, and
the words one hears are all absent, recorded:

> . . . a little rolled up perforated strip which "contains" vast
> landscapes, fixed battles, the melting of the ice on the River
> Neva, and whole life-times, and yet can be enclosed in the
> familiar round metal tin, of modest dimensions, clear proof that
> it does not "really" contain all that. (IS, p. 47)

Because of this "absence," this imaginary quality
of the signifier, Metz claims that "every film is a fiction
film" (IS, p. 47). However, unlike his work in *Film Language*
and *Language and Cinema* where he studied signification in terms
of the narrative-fiction film, in his linguistic-psychoanalytic approach he wishes to deal mainly with signification as it applies to cinema in general.

4. The "false" aspects of the perceptions of the
cinema in the sense that

> The activity of perception in it is real (the cinema is not
> fantasy), but the perceived is not really the object, it is its
> shade, its phantom, its double, its replica in a new kind of
> mirror. (IS, p. 48)

The next major section in "The Imaginary Signifier"
deals with the role of the spectator in the cinema and of
his relationship to the "mirror." Here Metz sees the factor
of identification operating on a number of levels:

1. The spectator identifies with the character of the
fiction in narrative-fictional films. However, according to
Metz, this type of identification is not valid for the

"psychoanalytic constitution of the signifier of the cinema as such" (IS, p. 49).

2. The spectator identifies with the actors or with the human figures appearing in films which do not employ actors.

3. The spectator identifies with himself. This comes about as a result of the place of the spectator's ego (in the Freudian-Lacanian sense) during the projection of the film.

The spectator is absent from the screen because the screen is not a true mirror since it does not reflect the spectator's image. Yet, the spectator is aware of two things: That he is perceiving something imaginary, and that he knows that it is he who is perceiving it. "In other words," Metz concludes, "the spectator identifies with himself" (IS, p. 50).

An important element in Lacan's psychoanalytic theory, which Metz incorporates in his work, is Lacan's concept of ego formation. According to Lacan the ego is founded on the opposition and identity between Self and Other: a child discovers that there is a difference between himself and the world and through the "imaginary" relationship to others this difference becomes an opposition. The child, which born as an undifferentiated "a-subjective" being, becomes an individual by passing through a phase during which it feels as "he" or "she" and eventually comes to feel as "I." The imaginary relationship to others centers around the Oedipus Complex. As the child matures and comes to feel as an individual this relationship becomes a symbolic one.[1]

The relationship between the child and the external world described above is somewhat similar to that described by Melanie Klein when she speaks of a "fantasy relationship" between the maturing individual and the external world.

4. The spectator identifies with the camera. During the showing of a film the projector replaces the camera. But, according to Metz, the projector is at the back of the spectator's head, "precisely where fantasy locates the 'focus' of all vision" (IS, p. 52).

5. The spectator identifies with the screen. To explain this aspect of identification Metz has to expand his theory of spectator identification with himself and the camera-projector. He claims that:

> During the performance the spectator is the searchlight . . . duplicating the projector, which itself duplicates the camera, and he is also the sensitive surface duplicating the screen, which itself duplicates the film-strip. (IS, p. 53)

In this manner, Metz claims, the cinematic signifier "depends on a series of mirror-effects organized in a chain" (IS, p. 53).

Metz is very insistent and quite defensive on this matter of a relationship to a mirror-like surface because, it seems, without it he cannot bring into his psychoanalytic approach the ego-formation mechanism which Freud and Lacan see as operating in life; which in turn may not allow him to deal with spectator identification in psychoanalytic terms at all.

What causes Metz to operate under stress is that he wants, once again, to be precise and "scientific," by utilizing this time the analogy that "film is like a mirror" (IS, p. 48), although he knows very well and admits that film "differs from the primordial mirror in one essential point . . . there is one thing, and one thing only that is never reflected in it: the spectator's own body" (IS, p. 48). Metz also knows that "the cinema spectator is not a child" (IS, p. 49). But since he is determined to build on this analogy although film is not a true mirror and the spectator is not a child, he claims that what makes possible "the intelligible unfolding of the film" is the fact that the spectator "has already known the experience of the mirror (of the true mirror), and is thus able to constitute a world of objects without first having to recognize himself within it" (IS, p. 49).

Since Metz wants to introduce to his scheme the dimension of the symbolic, which may allow him to incorporate in his work Lacan's ideas on the symbolic, he claims that the spectator "knows himself and he knows his like: it is no longer necessary that this similarity be literally depicted for him on the screen, as it was in the mirror of his childhood" (IS, p. 49). This, claims Metz, causes the cinema to be "on the side of the symbolic" (IS, p. 49).

A key weakness of this enterprise is that Metz provides no evidence whatsoever that what he is saying is based on any kind of research in the field of motion pictures or any of the other fields which are involved. Also, these impressions of his are not supported by any examples from films, or by the reactions which someone has had while viewing any specific film.

The importance of the analogy of the "mirror" becomes a very critical matter for Metz when he discusses certain "sub-codes of identification" which, according to him, operate in the cinema. Examples of such sub-codes are the various kinds of subjective shots, and various kinds of "looks." The unusual framings and uncommon angles, which are often associated with subjective shots, merely intensify the feeling of the spectator's identification with himself. As for "looks" (the way a character looks at someone else on the screen, or the point of view of a character indicated by a certain camera angle), Metz claims that they are related to the psychoanalytic concepts of "primary" and "secondary" identification which also play a role in ego formation.

In the cinema, Metz claims, identifying with one's own look must be considered "primary cinematic identification" (IS, p. 58), although in terms of Freudian and Lacanian psychoanalysis such identification constitutes secondary identification. On the other hand, Metz continues:

> . . . identification with the screen characters with their own
> levels (such as looks at out-of-frame characters or scenes which
> represent points of view of out-of-frame characters) represent
> secondary, tertiary cinematic identifications, and as such they
> are sub-codes. (IS, p. 58)

Only after he has prepared the ground in this manner
can Metz attempt to explain what is involved in the process
of signification as it operates in his linguistic-psychoanalytic approach to film communication. He describes the
process in this manner:

> . . . in order to understand the film (at all) I must perceive
> the photographed object as absent, its photograph as present, and
> the presence of this absence as signifying. The imaginary of the
> cinema presupposes the symbolic, for the spectator must first of
> all have known the primordial mirror. But as the latter insti-
> tuted the ego very largely in the imaginary, the second mirror
> of the screen, a symbolic apparatus, itself in turn depends on
> reflection and lack. However, it is not fantasy, a "purely"
> symbolic-imaginary site, for the absence of the object and the
> codes of that absence are really produced in it by the physis of
> an equipment: the cinema is a body (a corpus for the semiolo-
> gist), a fetish that can be loved. (IS, pp. 58-59)

With this reference to a fetish, Metz moves on to the
last two major sections of his essay where he discusses the
relationship between spectator and film in terms of
voyeurism and fetishism.

He claims that the cinema becomes possible through two
"perceptual passions" of a sexual nature: the desire to see
(scopic drive, scopophilia, voyeurism), and the desire to
hear (the "invocative drive") (IS, p. 59). Both of these
drives are dependent on a lack which marks them on the side
of the imaginary. This is so, we are told, because these
drives always remain more or less unsatisfied even when the

object of desire has been attained:

> The lack of what it wishes to fill, and at the same time what it is always careful to leave gaping, in order to survive as desire. In the end it has no object, at any rate no real object (a "lost object") which is its truest object, an object that has always been lost and is always desired as such. (IS, p. 60)

Metz associates all of this to Freud's observation that voyeurism always keeps apart the object looked at, and then he proceeds to build a case for the spectator relating to film in the manner of a voyeur. Then he goes on to associate cinematic voyeurism ("unauthorized scopophilia") with the concept of the "primal scene." To prove that such a relationship exists, he points to the following aspects of experiencing motion picture films:

1. The obscurity surrounding the onlooker-spectator during the projection of a film.

2. The keyhole effect of the screen aperture.

3. The less accepted and more shamefaced nature of cinematic voyeurism. This is due to the fact that, unlike the theatre which is an ancient art which grew out of ceremonial and religious practices giving a respectability to its voyeurism, the voyeurism of the cinema has not been accepted as "legitimate."

4. The manner in which the anonymous movie audiences enter and exit movie theatres has a "furtive" quality to it much like the visits to *maisons de tolerance*. The cinema, Metz claims,

> . . . is based on the legalization and generalization of the prohibited practice . . . going to the cinema is one licit

activity among others with its place in the admissible pastimes
of the day . . . and yet that place is a "hole" in the social
cloth, a loophole opening on to something slightly more crazy,
slightly less approved than what one does the rest of the time.
(IS, pp. 65-66)

The imaginary dimensions of the cinematic signifier,

and the voyeuristic aspects of the relationship between the

spectator and the projected film, are examined by Metz in

terms of exhibitionism. He observes that voyeurism rests on

the fiction that the object of the voyeur's attention

"agrees" to be observed and it is, therefore, practicing a

form of exhibitionism. But, unlike the theatre where the

spectator and the actor are at the same time present one to

another, in the cinema:

. . . the actor was present when the spectator was not (=shooting),
and the spectator is present when the actor is no longer (=projec-
tion): a failure to meet of the voyeur and the exhibitionist
whose approaches no longer coincide (they have "missed" one
another). The cinema's voyeurism must (of necessity) do without
any very clear mark of consent on the part of the object. (IS,
p. 63)

One of the most important "roots" of the cinema in the

unconscious mind, which justifies a psychoanalytic approach

to cinematic signification, is, according to Metz, the

fetishistic aspects of the relationship between the specta-

tor and the film. Metz informs us that for Freud and Lacan

fetishism is linked very closely with castration and the

fear which castration inspires. Embracing the classic

Freudian views on the subject and the shift toward the

symbolic aspects of castration as expounded by Lacan, Metz

points out the following:

1. Castration is the mother's castration who, according to the child, has lost her penis.

2. The terrified child attempts to "arrest its look" at what becomes its fetish. The fetish is a negative signifier and represents the penis. It is always a substitute for it.

3. The cinematic aspects of fetishism include film equipment and film technique, the enchantment for the cinema shown by the film connoisseur, the pleasure derived by the moviegoer, and the desire of the film theoretician to write about film (IS, pp. 71-73).

Metz closes "The Imaginary Signifier" by stating in very lyrical terms that

> Psychoanalysis does not illuminate only the film, but also the conditions of desire of whoever makes himself its theoretician. Interwoven into every analytical undertaking is the thread of self-analysis. (IS, p. 75)

From the Linguistic to the Linguistic-Psychoanalytic Approach

The following brief comments, relating Metz's earlier linguistic approach to the linguistic-psychoanalytic, seem to be necessary for a proper transition to the last part of this chapter which deals with the psychoanalytic approach and the reality of film.

In "The Imaginary Signifier," Metz admits that, compared to a more classical semiological approach such as the one he had attempted earlier, in a psychoanalytic approach attention shifts from the *énoncé* to the *énonciation*;

from what is uttered to the act of uttering.

This shift drives Metz away from the isolation of a "filmic object" which can be studied phenomenologically. However, he does not appear willing to abandon his search for such an "object." "The Imaginary Signifier" is full of references to the "manifest content" of films which serve as the "object" of study. Exactly what is the nature of the "manifest content" of films is never made clear.

An equally vague term which he uses often is "manifest filmic material." This material is said to have signifiers and signifieds. As indicated earlier, Metz's psychoanalytic approach deals with "the matter of the signifier" of this manifest filmic material and with the codes which are allowed by the "pertinent features" of the signifier (IS, p. 42). Exactly what these "pertinent features" happen to be is never explained.

As for the codes which these mysterious "pertinent features" allow, the impression is given that the codes could be properties of these features and not creations of the analyst. Here Metz seems to be engaging again in the same deceptive practice which characterized *Language and Cinema* by making the codes appear to be either properties of the manifest cinematic material, or analytic tools; depending on what best suits his purpose at a given point in the analysis.

The distinction between the "filmic" and the "cinematic" which was attempted unsuccessfully in *Film Language* and in *Language and Cinema*, is attempted again in "The Imaginary Signifier." Metz indicates that his psychoanalytic approach will be applied to the cinematic.

Although he has never been able to make a convincing case for a distinction and a difference between the signifier and the signified in the cinema, he proceeds here to utilize this distinction, and he points out that his purpose is to study psychoanalytically the cinematic signifier and not the signified.

In *Film Language* the purpose of his study was to examine the narrative fiction film. In *Language and Cinema* his analytic procedures were meant for the narrative fiction film and for other types of films. In "The Imaginary Signifier" Metz tries to establish an approach which is suitable for the analysis of the cinematic signifier in general because, as he hints, the process of signification is identical in the various types of films and film genres.[2] However, he provides no evidence whatsoever that this observation about the process of signification is based on a formal study of any kind.

Metz claims that psychoanalysis explores the "primary process," and linguistics (and modern symbolic logic) the "secondary process." Together they cover the entire field of signification (IS, p. 28). "Primary processes" are the experiences, resulting from frustrations, which stimulate

130

the development of the Id. "Secondary processes" are the
activities of the Ego through which reality is discovered
and produced by means of action developed by thought and
reason.[3]

There are important links between linguistics and
psychoanalysis. But, it seems to me, the claim that
psychoanalysis deals with the "primary process" and linguistics with the "secondary process," a claim made so that
these two fields can be combined in the study of cinematic
signification, represents an over-simplification and a
distortion of what these two fields explore. An elaborate
case could be made questioning the wisdom and validity of
linking the two fields in the manner in which Metz links
them in order to study the cinematic signifier. Such a
"case" falls outside the limits of this study. However, it
should be pointed out here that Metz's method of linking
these two fields consists of applying to the examination of
the cinematic signifier a mixture of linguistic and psychoanalytic methods, principles, and concepts, without provid-
ing any evidence whatsoever that the methods, principles,
and concepts of these two fields (of any two fields) can be
combined in this manner. One is tempted to remind Metz of
what he said in *Language and Cinema* about such an uncritical
blending of analytic techniques:

> Methods are things which cannot be interchanged and which cannot
> be "combined" without great danger of giving rise to monstrocit-
> ies. (LC, p. 20)

131

What makes Metz's mixture of linguistics and psychoanalysis particularly disturbing is that he attempts to
incorporate in it the ideas and writing style of Jacques
Lacan.

Lacan is perhaps the most controversial writer in the
field of psychoanalysis who is suspected of making his
writings impossible to understand as a matter of conscious
intellectual strategy.[4]

Characteristic of the reaction which Lacan evokes are
the views of Anthony Wilden. In his impressive study
System and Structure, Wilden says that Lacan's works

> . . . read more like a "schizophrenic discourse"--or like poetry,
> or nonsense, depending on your prejudice and your tendencies
> towards positive or negative transference--than anything else.
> Lacan's hermeticism cannot be excused on any grounds.[5]

Lacan's overall "scientific" method is described by
Wilden in this manner:

> Lacan takes bits and pieces from everywhere and anywhere and
> jumbles them up--like the text of a dream--playing on ambiguities,
> etymologies, puns, analogies, poetic metaphors--again like the
> text of a dream--as well as on the reader's benevolent desire to
> understand. Lacan's argument is presumably that he is represent-
> ing his theory in the very "language" the theory is designed to
> analyze: if you understand the theory, you will then understand
> his exposition, and vice versa. Within all this, there appear
> strikingly important concepts, such as the theory of the Imagin-
> ary. Such an attitude nevertheless defies the simplest criterion
> of all "science": that any theory must be demonstrably less
> complex than what it is intended to explain.[6]

Even Claude Lévi-Strauss, from whom Lacan has borrowed
key elements of the structural linguistic approach, attacks
some of Lacan's major positions as being "imposture" and
"sleight of hand."[7]

The result of this reliance on the ideas and writing style of a writer such as Lacan is that Metz describes the function of the psychoanalytic approach, which "The Imaginary Signifier" represents, in terms which often defy comprehension.

As for the influence of Melanie Klein on Metz's approach, in "The Imaginary Signifier" it is limited to certain relatively minor concepts such as the "good" and "bad object" relationship between a subject and an object. However, Metz saying that the spectator has a "good" or a "bad object" relationship with a film, instead of saying that the spectator liked or disliked a film, hardly amounts to a contribution of psychoanalysis to our understanding of how films communicate.

The Linguistic-Psychoanalytic Approach and the Reality of Film

It has been indicated that "The Imaginary Signifier" represents Metz's attempt to set the foundations of his new linguistic-psychoanalytic approach. This approach is still in the process of being developed. For this reason, "The Imaginary Signifier" must be viewed in terms of establishing the direction towards which Metz is heading and not in term of specific achievements made possible by this approach.

Examined from the point of view of the reality of film, this essay reveals that Metz basically does not plan to develop anything other than a psychoanalytically flavored reinterpretation of the signification process which he described in *Film Language* and *Language and Cinema*. This appears to be the case because his "psychoanalytic inspiration" turns out to be not a real integration of psychoanalysis and film, but a labeling with psychoanalytic jargon of certain aspects of his earlier structural linguistic approach.

The similarity between his earlier approach and the new psychoanalytic one is also demonstrated by the fact that in "The Imaginary Signifier" the reality of film is acknowledged and then disregarded. Since the pattern of this practice has been demonstrated in the previous chapters there is no need here to give examples of how Metz acknowledges and then disregards the reality of film. Instead, what follows is a brief presentation of what occurs in this essay in terms of the various aspects of the reality of film.

The Director as the Author of the Film

In "The Imaginary Signifier" the banishment of the director as the author of the film is as complete as in *Film Language* and in *Language and Cinema*. This is so despite the fact that Metz claims that in a psychoanalytic approach attention shifts from *énoncé* to *énonciation*. Concern for the spectator as a participant in the act of *énonciation* appears to be an important part of the new approach. However, concern for the director as a participant in the "act of saying" is replaced by concern for the role of the analyst.

What banishes the author/director is Metz's determination to avoid the "nosographic" and the "psychologically inspired characterology" type of approach. As we have seen, these approaches are rejected because they are indifferent to the "filmic text."

Apparently, Metz fails to see that his claim that the psychoanalytic approach shifts attention from énoncé to énonciation, is in conflict with his claim that what needs to be studied psychoanalytically is the "filmic text" which is clearly an énoncé.

An additional reason given for the rejection of the "nosographic" and "psychological characterology" types of approaches is that, according to Metz, they remain indifferent to the social aspects of signification (IS, p. 33). Metz is clearly in error here because most of the studies of this nature view the neuroses and other aspects of the personality of the author/director in a sociocultural perspective.

In his discussion of sub-codes of identification, such as "subjective images" which express the viewpoint of the filmmaker, it seems that Metz places himself in the position of having to deal with the author/director as an important element in the process of signification.

However, Metz extricates himself from this situation by resorting to a manipulation of Lacanian psychoanalysis which permits him to deal only with the spectator and maintain the banishment of the author. The following description of how the spectator supposedly feels when confronted with "subjective images" is characteristic of the dexterity by which Metz manages to stay on course with his approach:

> Precisely because it is uncommon, the uncommon angle makes us more aware of what we had merely forgotten to some extent in its absence: an identification with the camera (with "the author's viewpoint"). The ordinary framings are really felt to be non-framings: I espouse the film-maker's look...but my consciousness is not too aware of it. The uncommon angle reawakens me and (like the cure) teaches me what I already knew. And then, it obliges my look to stop wandering freely over the screen for the moment and to scan it along more precise lines of force which are imposed on me. Thus for a moment I become directly aware of the placement of my own presence-absence in the film simply because it has changed. (IS, pp. 56-57)

Beyond this point in "The Imaginary Signifier," Metz avoids any discussion which deals with aspects of signification which may involve the author of the film.

The Relationship Between Spectator and Film

Unlike *Film Language* and *Language and Cinema,* where Metz had practically nothing to say about this relationship because the object of his investigation was not really the filmophanic film, "The Imaginary Signifier" contains extensive material on the relationship between spectator and film. These are the sections where Metz talks about the nature of the "perceptual passions" of sight and hearing, the aspects of voyeurism in film viewing, and the disavowal-fetishism involved in seeing and writing about films.

The length of these sections, amounting to approximately

half the material in the essay, and the detail in which he describes the relationship, give the impression that Metz finally intends to deal with this aspect of the reality of film in a meaningful way. However, both the length and the intricacy of the material are deceptive as far as a significant contribution to our understanding of how films communicate is concerned.

The element of deception in Metz's work is contained in two aspects of his presentation: (a) What he has to say about the relationship between the spectator and film is not related to the announced aim of his new approach which is the examination of the cinematic signifier in terms of Hjelmslev's ideas, and (b) his approach indicates a great lack of critical distance from Freudian psychoanalysis.

The relationship described in the sections which deal with perception, voyeurism, and fetishism, is that between a human being, the spectator, and the filmophanic film. The relationship suggested in the statement of purpose of the psychoanalytic approach to film, concerns a relationship between an analyst such as Metz and analytic concepts which are the creations of the analyst; it is a study of the matter of the signifier in Hjelmslev's sense.

In this mixture of approaches no pattern exists, no criteria, and, in the final analysis, no apparent logic for all the mental acrobatics involved in his talking about a spectator's relationship to the filmophanic film in one

paragraph, and an analyst's relationship to the matter of
the signifier in another paragraph.

The lack of critical distance from Freudian psychoanalysis which characterizes the psychoanalytic dimension of
Metz's new approach has been the subject of harsh criticism
from a number of quarters.[8] This lack of critical distance
appears to stem from Metz's assumption that psychoanalysis
is a science, and from the assumption that the methods of
interpretation of a patient's responses to the probing of a
psychoanalyst can be applied to the analysis of a spectator's reactions to films. However, in the case of cinema,
Metz does not have the benefit of the responses of the film,
the author of the film, or the spectator.

In view of all this, what Metz has to say in "The
Imaginary Signifier" about the guilt-ridden spectator/voyeur
who is secretly entering movie theatres as if visiting
brothels in a symbolic search for his lost penis, may be
illuminating in terms of coming to know Christian Metz but
not of how films communicate. Metz has again ended up in a
dialogue with himself.

Film Content and the
Linguistic-Psychoanalytic
Approach

When Metz talks about the spectator relating to the
screen as if to a mirror-like surface through which rapport
is established with a Lacanian symbolic "other," he is
suggesting that the spectator relates to a content of films

138

which consists of images and sounds that make up a motion picture film. He is suggesting that a relationship exists with what I have identified in this study as an important aspect of the reality of film.

However, this is another of the deceptive qualities of Metz's work. The "content" which his linguistic-psycho-analytic approach actually sets out to investigate is the matter of the signifier in Hjelmslev's sense.

Here it must be noted that Hjelmslev claims that language manifests itself on three basic levels: form, matter (or purport), and substance.[9] Form is the pure network of relations which define a set of elements. Matter is the initially amorphous instance in which form is manifested. Substance is the configuration which is obtained by inscribing form in matter.

These levels of language are examined by Hjelmslev in terms of another major distinction: expression-content. Expression and content are designations of the functives of the linguistic sign. The entity called the linguistic sign is generated by the union between expression and content. Expression and content necessarily presuppose each other. An expression is expression only by being a content of expression.

Then, form, matter, and substance are related to expression and content, allowing Hjelmslev to distinguish in language six fundamental levels: form of expression, form

of content, matter of expression, matter of content, substance of expression, and substance of content.[10]

Armed with such distinctions and levels, Hjelmslev
moves into even more abstract territory employing a maze of
terminological innovations in which he fails to show the
relevance of all these distinctions in describing a real
language.[11] Hjelmslev's concept of language as a purely
deductive system and his inconsistent use of an extravagant
and forbidding terminology has been criticized rather
severely, especially by American linguists.[12]

For his new approach, Metz takes Hjelmslev's concept of
language, his terminology, and his distinctions, and applies
to them Jacques Lacan's version of Sigmund Freud's
psychoanalytic concepts and procedures.

In "The Imaginary Signifier" Metz provides no clues
whatsoever on how this concoction of Hjelmslev-Lacan-Freud
will deal with the images and sounds making up the content
of motion picture films shown in movie theatres. If Metz
does not intend to deal with this aspect of the reality of
film, where do his comments about the voyeur/spectator fit
in his new approach? One has great difficulty imagining
how a search for the lost penis can be accomplished in
Hjelmslev's sense.

The Film As Art

It is obvious that in "The Imaginary Signifier" Metz
is not interested in examining film as an art form. But,

in applying psychoanalytic concepts to film he is forced to deal with a subject which has been one of the major concerns of traditional film aesthetics: the framed movie image and the spectator's relationship to it.

Realist and formalist approaches to traditional film aesthetics have used metaphors such as "window," "mask," and "frame" in describing the functions of the photographed/ projected image. Thus, the movie mask/frame has been regarded, among other things, as a device for editing, delimiting, organizing, composing, and ordering reality for the benefit of the spectator.

Metz adds to the extensive literature on this subject new metaphors and analogies and he examines the spectator's response in terms of such devices. His contribution is the concept of the movie frame (the screen image) as a "mirror" in the Lacanian sense, and the "imaginary relationship" between the spectator and what is reflected in the "mirror" as a kind of dream.

This seems to be an important contribution and a step in a useful direction. Finally, Metz appears to come to grips with the reality of film.

Unfortunately, upon closer examination this does not prove to be the case.

Through the concept of the mirror and the "imaginary relationship" of the spectator, Metz is merely re-stating in terms of Lacan's concepts and terminology what has been

examined in traditional film aesthetics as far back as 1916.
Generations of writers on the cinema, including such names
as Hugo Munsterberg, Ilya Ehrenburg, Hugo Mauerhofer, and
Suzanne Langer, have spoken of the dream-like quality of the
relationship between the spectator and projected film: the
relative passivity of the spectator in the darkened theatre
which brings about a receptiveness which induces a
suspension and a withdrawal from reality during which the
unreal is somehow accepted in a way as real.

It is true, of course, that the conventional approaches
to film aesthetics have left many questions unanswered. For
example, exactly what is involved in the heightened
receptiveness of the spectator and how that which is
obviously (logically) unreal comes to be accepted as real
has never been explained in a very satisfactory manner. It
is also true that the works of the conventional approach
to film aesthetics very often contain passages which are
too lyrical and "impressionistic."

But, stripped of its Lacanian psychoanalytic jargon
and rephrased in more conventional terms, Metz's approach
adds nothing to what has been said already about film as
an art form. Metz merely better disguises his "impressionism."

Since reference has been made to Metz's metaphors of
the screen image being a "mirror," and the spectator's
experience being a "dream," it must be pointed out again

142

that the entire linguistic dimension of Metz's work is based on the analogy that film is like a language. Metz's problems are those of a man who attempts to develop a science which is based on analogies and metaphors.

The Individual Film As a Unique Determination

In *Film Language* Metz proclaimed that the image is a *hapax*, a unique determination, and that it is not possible to create a "dictionary" of images since there is an infinite number of them. In *Language and Cinema* he admitted that the codes tell us nothing about the film as a whole and he proceeded to demonstrate that what accounts for a film's organizing principles is the textual system. This system is a unique mixture of codes and as such it is unrepeatable. The manner in which these codes combine to form the unique system was something which Metz failed to determine. His failure prevented him from dealing in any meaningful manner with "filmic writing," the last major undertaking in *Language and Cinema*, and seriously weakened the value of the codes as keys to cinematic signification.

Certainly, counting and recounting codes within a film is not a very productive undertaking because codes are keyboards and of themselves they indicate nothing about how they can be used to produce meaning. In the absence of a system for knotting these codes into the unique systems which make up the individual film, the codes cannot help

143

us deal with signification as it applies to the complete film.[13]

In "The Imaginary Signifier" Metz tries to establish a case for codes of the dream but again he fails to indicate how these codes combine to account for the film as a whole.

Freud, to whom Metz has turned for assistance, is not of much help when it comes to accounting for the uniqueness of a given work of film art. This is so because Freud was unable to explain how the process of displacements (replacement of blocked object-cathexes with substitutes) often leads to what he called a "sublimation"; the deflection of psychic energy into the creation of works or the pursuit of other intellectual goals.[14] For Freud "sublimation" remained a mystery, the mystery of creation. For Metz the sublimation of the codes of the dream into meaningful and unique works of cinema also remains a mystery. But, unlike Freud, who admitted his inability to explain sublimation, Metz remains absolutely silent about this very serious flaw of his analytic procedure.

What makes Metz's silence on this matter even more disturbing is his eloquence on the subject of changing his mind about the existence of textual systems in films. He announces that one of the contributions of psychoanalysis to linguistics is that he no longer believes that each film has a textual system, or even a fixed number of such systems as he claimed in *Language and Cinema*. In fact, the

144

concept of the textual system seems to be abandoned. Now
he sees the existence of a kind of "working conveniences,"
or "sorts of blocks of interpretation" which constitutes a
new kind of infinitely "thick" textual systems which are
created by the analysis as a result of a mysterious force
labelled by Metz "significatory pressure" (IS, p. 50).

The result of this change in Metz's procedures is that
now there is nothing left to account for the uniqueness of
the individual film. Not even the mystery of creation!
Everything has come now under the control of the analyst.
The codes are his creation and so is the system. The
analyst does not care to explain how the codes combine to
create the system. There is only the matter of the
"significatory pressure" as a faint ray of hope that something exists which may be independent of the analyst. But
Metz is very cryptic about this "pressure" and he drops the
subject after mentioning it only twice.

The Sociocultural Roots of Film

The introduction of psychoanalysis to the structural
linguistic approach for the study of cinematic signification
could loosen upon Metz's method the "myriad winds of culture" which he avoided so carefully in *Film Language* and
Language and Cinema. This is so because Freud related the
development of the human psyche to a large number of
sociocultural influences, and because he incorporated in
his psychoanalytic procedures numerous insights on the

145

nature of artistic activity which point to the social

function of art.[15]

The social function of art, as perceived by Freud,

involves the

> . . . transmission of the artist's ideas and psychic states by the
> use of symbols capable of carrying both conscious and unconscious
> stimuli which together evoke in the appreciator a combined
> intellectual and emotional response. Their power is enhanced by
> their patterns (artistic form) especially when these approximate
> the patterns of the basic human experiences which both artist and
> audience have as their common heritage.[16]

Some key concepts of Freudian psychoanalysis which deal

with the relationship between the individual and the exter-

nal world are those of Ego, Superego, Dream, the Reality

Principle, and Identification. Ego is the psychological

system which is governed by the "reality principle" and

which transacts between the person and the outside world.

Superego is the moral and judicial dimension of personality.

It develops out of the child's assimilation of his parents'

standards, and enables the person to control his behavior

and adjust it to what is socially acceptable. The impulses

most often controlled by the Superego are those of sex and

aggression because they are considered to be the most

dangerous to the stability of society. A dream is a

succession of mental images having as its function the

reduction of tension by reviving memories of past events and

objects associated with the gratifications of needs. The

"reality principle" is a mechanism of the Ego through which,

in the interest of reality, there is a postponement in the

discharge of energy towards the satisfaction of needs until
the actual object, which will be able to satisfy the needs,
has been discovered or produced. Serving the "reality
principle" is the "secondary process" which consists of
discovering reality through a plan or action developed by
thought and reason. Identification is the incorporation of
the qualities of another person into one's personality. A
very common type is "goal-oriented identification" where a
frustrated individual achieves vicarious satisfaction by
identifying with someone who is successful in reaching his
goals.

Freud's analysis of the sociocultural aspects of
artistic activity examined the frame of mind of the artist,
the manner in which the artist's vision is reflected in the
work of art, and the nature of the relationship between the
artist and the appreciator of works of art.

In terms of the reality of film, it seems that a
complete and proper utilization of Freudian psychoanalysis
in the study of cinematic signification should take into
account all of the important elements involved in the communication process: artist, work of art, appreciator of
the work of art, and social setting.

However, in his linguistic-psychoanalytic approach Metz
banishes the artist/author, does not treat film as art, and
he ignores the social setting. Also, he substitutes the
analyst for the appreciator/spectator, focuses only on

selected psychoanalytic concepts, and then he manipulates these concepts out of context of the Freudian-Lacanian approach in order to retreat into the dialectical abstractions of structural linguistics.

Of interest in this section is that Metz manipulates certain psychoanalytic concepts and that this act eliminates the sociocultural roots of the cinema. This manipulation is most evident in connection with the analogies of Screen/Mirror and Film/Dream.

A major problem seems to be that Metz cannot claim that the projected movie image is a true mirror in the Freudian-Lacanian sense. He admits this and explains in considerable detail the many ways in which the screen image is not a mirror. But, since he insists on using this psychoanalytic concept without being able to refer to a relationship with a mirror, he builds an elaborate case for the analogy of the screen image being *like* a mirror.

The relationship of the individual with the mirror, as described by Lacan, occurs within a sociocultural setting and accounts for the development of the ego and the sense of identity which a person has as a social being.

Metz claims that the relationship between the spectator and the mirror-like screen is a very special one. The spectator, he says, has already known the true mirror and his ego is formed. The screen/mirror has nothing to do with the ability of the spectator, in terms of real life, to make the transition from the imaginary to what Lacan calls the "symbolic" level.

The analogy of the mirror-like screen is manipulated by Metz so that he can prove that the spectator identifies with himself. This, in turn, is used by him to point out that while the spectator is in this frame of mind signification in the cinema springs out of the "presence" of the spectator perceiving the photographed (and projected) object as absent.

From this point on the "psychoanalytic inspiration" is discarded and Metz lapses into familiar structural linguistic methodology. Close examination of the path which he takes in order to arrive at the conclusion that signification is generated out of the presence of perceiving something as absent indicates that he could have achieved the same result without the aid of psychoanalytic concepts. In this respect the use of psychoanalysis is entirely superficial and deceptive. Metz is merely decorating with psychoanalytic jargon what he has said numerous times in *Film Language* and *Language and Cinema*.

The Screen-Mirror analogy as used by Metz does not permit him to indicate how social influences and aspects of culture can be reflected in the projected film, and how the spectator (or even the analyst) can relate to them. Metz's failure to deal with the sociocultural aspects of the reality of film is very disappointing in view of the fact

that Lacan, with his emphasis on symbolic aspects of signification, offers him an opportunity to involve this reality.
It is true that Metz mentions a number of times that in
viewing a film the spectator makes the transition from an
imaginary to a symbolic level. But Metz does not indicate
how this occurs or what features of the perceived film
allow the spectator to make this transition.

As indicated earlier, Metz claims that films are *like*
a dream and that the spectator relates to them as if
relating to a dream. Metz even claims that as a film
theorist he relates to the linguistic-psychoanalytic
approach as if relating to a dream. He says, for example,
that the central question which "The Imaginary Signifier"
tries to answer is a dream/question. He also claims that
the entire essay is the interpretation of that dream/
question and that he examines the matters of "contribution,"
"Freudian," and "cinematic signifier" by associating freely
between them by following the method suggested by Freud in
his works on dream interpretation (IS, p. 28).

In the passages where he talks about aspects of
voyeurism and fetishism in the relationship between the
spectator and film, Metz engages in a rather extensive
analysis of his own "dream" of wanting to examine cinematic
signification. The "textual system," which becomes the
target of his investigation, is claimed to possess a
"latent" quality which, according to Freud, operates on

both the unconscious and the preconscious level. Therefore, this latent quality of the "textual system" must be subjected to analysis and interpretation similar to the one applied to dreams (IS, p. 38).

This dream approach to film theory is disappointing in terms of the sociocultural aspects of the reality of film because Metz rejects the "dream analysis" of all the aspects of film which are in any way related to what he calls "the story." This eliminates the analysis of the images and sounds that make up a film along with characters, events, settings, time periods, and the orchestration of these elements. All of this is rejected because, according to Metz, "the story" is "indifferent to the cinematic signifier" (IS, p. 40).

Since Metz has never been able to present a convincing case that there can be a distinction in the cinema between signifier and signified, one could argue that "the story" is not merely a signified and it cannot be rejected for purposes of dream analysis. Of course, Metz's dialectical polarities and transformations do not permit arguments of this kind. The circularity of his approach permits him to accept everything and nothing and to proceed in any direction he chooses to proceed.

However, with "the story" eliminated from dream analysis, he is unable to deal with anything which is associated with matters of ideology. By "ideology" what is meant is

not just political orientation but the system of ideas and
connotations which human beings build up and which provide
them with a sense of direction in life and a guide for their
actions.[17] To put it in psychoanalytic terms, ideology is
the orientation provided to the individual by the Superego.

Specifically, Metz's dream analysis is unable to deal
with the following aspects of what is called here ideology:

1. Transmitted and inherited through the family group
aspects of ideology.

2. Social group and social standing aspects of
ideology.

3. Ethnic and racial identity aspects of ideology.

4. Political and religious aspects of ideology.

5. Features of ideology which are related to period
in history.

6. Features of ideology which are related to geo-
graphic location.

7. Sexual identity aspects of ideology.

8. "Technical" aspects of ideologies such as their
high degree of dependence on inner evidence and rejection of
empirical proof, their durability, and their inflexibility.

9. Aesthetic aspects of ideologies such as people's
concepts on the nature of beauty, pleasure, etc.

Despite the rejection of all of the above dimensions of
ideology, in his dream analysis Metz does focus upon
something which is related to the reality of life and the
reflection of that reality in ideology: the sexual act and
152

the concerns which human beings have in connection with it.

The problem is that Metz gives the impression that the sexual act is not just the most important element in human existence, but the *only* one which is relevant in connection with cinematic signification.

It is true that Freud believed that all dreams contain a very large number of disguised representations of repressed sexual needs and images of the tension-reducing objects which represent wish-fulfillments. But, to make the sexual act, and the "complexes" which Freud associated with it, the most important element in dream analysis and the key to cinematic signification, represents a distorted view of the Freudian approach and an embarrassingly naïve proposition as to where the heart of cinematic signification lies.

The great reliance on the analysis of sexual matters seems inappropriate for another reason which has to do with the structural linguistic aspect of Metz's approach. The search for the lost penis, literal or symbolic, is related to the thematic material of the rejected dimension of "the story," and not to the matter of the signifier in Hjelmslev's sense.

FOOTNOTES

[1] Anthony Wilden, *System and Structure* (London: Tavistock, 1972), p. 261.

[2] Metz, "The Imaginary Signifier," pp. 41-42, 45.

[3] Calvin Hall, *A Primer of Freudian Psychology* (New York: World Publishing Co., 1963), pp. 24-29.

[4] Buscombe, et al., "Psychoanalysis and Film," p. 120.

[5] Wilden, *System and Structure*, pp. 5-6.

[6] Wilden, pp. 14-15.

[7] Buscombe, et al., "Psychoanalysis and Film," p. 120.

[8] For example, see Julia LeSage, "The Human Subject: You, He, or Me?" *Screen*, 16, No. 2 (Summer, 1975), 77-82.

[9] Louis Hjelmslev, *Prolegomena to a Theory of Language*, Revised English Edition (Madison: University of Wisconsin Press, 1969).

[10] Stephen Heath, "Metz's Semiology: A Short Glossary," *Screen*, 14, No. 1/2 (Spring/Summer, 1973), 222.

[11] R. R. K. Hartmann, *The Language of Linguistics* (Tübingen: Tübinger Beiträge zur Linguistik, 1973), pp. 57-59.

[12] David Crystal, *Linguistics* (Harmondsworth: Penguin, 1971), p. 246.

[13] J. Dudley Andrew, "Film Analysis or Film Therapy: To Step Beyond Semiotics," *Quarterly Review of Film Studies*, 2, No. 1 (February, 1977), 33-41.

[14] Hall, *Primer of Freudian Psychology*, pp. 82-83.

[15] References to the nature of artistic activity appear throughout his works. In addition to these references, Freud conducted studies on Dostoevsky, Goether, Leonardo da Vinci, and Shakespear.

[16] Louis Fraiberg, *Psychoanalysis and American Literary Criticism* (Detroit: Wayne State University Press, 1960), 44-45.

[17] Paul Schilder, *Psychoanalysis, Man, and Society* (New York: W. W. Norton & Co., 1951), 61.

SUMMARY AND CONCLUSIONS

Christian Metz is considered to be one of the most important film theoreticians of our times, who has made great contributions towards the establishment of a scientific approach to the study of how films communicate. Speaking of his own work Metz has declared that he intervened in the course of film studies in order to help eliminate the impressionistic excesses of conventional film criticism and theory.

To achieve the task which he set for himself, Metz initially attempted to apply to the study of film communication the principles of structural linguistics on the assumption that film is a kind of language. After more than a decade of efforts along this line, he turned to an approach which combines structural linguistic theory and psychoanalysis. This time the added assumptions were that the unconscious mind is structured like a language and that film is like a dream.

The purpose of this study was to determine to what extent Metz has contributed something of value towards our understanding of how films communicate; something which indeed eliminates the alleged impressionistic excesses of

155

conventional film theory. To deal with this problem I felt that Metz's work should be confronted with "the reality of film" as it pertains to the fiction narrative film which has been the focus of Metz's investigations.

The basic elements of this reality are that film is an art, that individual films have an author, and that they are cultural objects to which an audience relates on a personal level and as part of social interaction.

The uniqueness and significance of this study hopefully lies in that an attempt was made to examine fairly closely three important works by Metz in order to determine whether or not Metz really studies film and not something which he claims to be film when in reality it is not. The reason for taking this approach was the suspicion that the basic assumptions on which Metz bases his investigations inevitably lead him to an analysis of something which is not film, with the result that his work does not contribute anything of value to our understanding of how films communicate.

In this study an attempt was made to confront Metz with his own words through extensive quotes which indicate that he is fully aware of the reality of film. This was done to focus attention on a certain pattern which was discerned in his works involving an acknowledgement of the reality of film followed by the manipulation of the elements he borrows from structural linguistics and psychoanalysis for the development of analytic procedures which do not

156

permit him to deal with this reality.

The fairly extensive quotes from his works were also thought to be necessary because I felt that a considerable number of the existing studies and references to his work exhibited a lack of concern for the inconsistencies and flaws of his analytic procedures. As a result, most of these existing studies and references have probably exaggerated the importance of Metz's contribution to film theory, and they may have been detrimental to the work of those who have depended on these studies in conducting their own investigations and analyses of films.

In the opening remarks of the first chapter, which was entitled "The Tortured Mind," I pointed out the reasons for Metz's "intervention," and I tried to describe what Metz sees as his goal in creating analytic procedures which were based initially on structural linguistics and later on, linguistics and psychoanalysis. A second section in that chapter consisted of extensive quotes from the primary sources for this study which indicate Metz's awareness of the reality of film. The major portion of that chapter dealt with some very disturbing features of Metz's overall approach and style which explain in part why he is unable to deal with the reality of film.

All of these difficulties seem to stem from the fact that in *Film Language* and in *Language and Cinema* Metz bases his approach on the analogy that film is a kind of language, and then he proceeds to use the concepts and methods which apply to the study of language in order to develop his analytic procedures. The fact that film is not a language and that there are very fundamental differences between film and language, which Metz acknowledges fully, places him in a very difficult position and imposes upon his supposedly precise and scientific procedures an impressionistic quality which is very similar to the one he attempted to eliminate with his "intervention." Considering that Metz has a very good background in film theory and criticism and that he seems to be an intelligent and sensitive person, it is quite astonishing that he fails to realize how imprecise and impressionistic his approach turns out to be.

Especially in *Film Language,* Metz seems to be literally in an agonized state of mind battling against the windmills of his own creation. Chapter I attempts to point to the great uncertainty, timidity, hesitancy, vagueness, and circularity of his thought. The chapter also gives examples of some of the impossible distinctions which he attempts to make, and some of the problems he encounters by an outpouring of neologisms and by creating numerous and intersecting elements, levels, and ranks for models of a whole which he never constructs.

Since his *Grande Syntagmatique* is supposed to be one of his major achievements, this chapter includes a number of comments on this model of the major analytic units for the

examination of cinematic intelligibility. As I pointed
out, this model is incomplete in that it cannot account
for all possible types of syntagmatic relationships, it
is applicable to certain epochs only in the development of
film, and in general, it seems to be nothing more than a
presentation in linguistic jargon of types of shots and of
relationships between shots which have been discussed in
the works of the conventional film theorists decades before
Metz appeared on the scene.

As far as his impossible distinctions is concerned, it
seems that the most troublesome are those of denotation/
connotation, cinematic/filmic, and code/message. Metz is
simply unable to establish that there can be valid distinctions between these elements. And yet, he bases much of
what he is attempting to do in *Film Language* and *Language and
Cinema* on these impossible distinctions.

The major reason for his difficulties in this area
seems to be that, as far as the motion picture image is
concerned, he cannot establish that it is possible to
distinguish between denotation and connotation. The same
seems to apply to the sound track elements although he does
not examine the problems of the sound track in any detail.

Unable to focus properly on the object of his study,
and influenced by what he considers to be methodological
features of structural linguistics and of the dialectical
approach, Metz examines matters through what I call a

"drifting" point of view. In this approach the study of
cinematic signification acquires ~the flavor of an intellectual game with a seemingly infinite number of continuously
changing rules. In this game, the reader is almost always
asked to go along with whatever argument Metz is presenting
and not to pay attention to disturbing contradictions and
inconsistencies. Metz simply asks us to have faith in him
and to trust that improvements will come about in some
unspecified time in the future.

This chapter also deals briefly with two more very
disturbing qualities of Metz's overall style: His proof
via manifesto and the lyrical quality of his writing. The
almost total lack of documentation which plagues his work
when it comes to supplying evidence that signification in
motion pictures occurs as described by him, is concealed by
the fact that he presents the premises of structual linguistics as self-evident truths. In this manner trying to deal
with Metz is equivalent to engaging in an argument with a
religious zealot. Coupled with what is a very obvious
quality of self-affectation in all of his writings, this
proof via manifesto technique and the accompanying lyrical
style give to his works the quality and flavor not of
scholarship but of some sort of fiction or poetry.

The second chapter of this study, "From Movies to
Cine-Text," deals with Metz's "reduction" of film into
something which is unrelated to the "filmophanic film"; the

film as experienced by the spectator during projection.

Metz's "reduction" takes the form of banishing the film author, of failing to take into account the content of the filmophanic film, and of constructing and dealing with a product of his mind which has nothing to do with what an audience perceives on the screen during the projection of a motion picture film.

The interesting and at the same time very deceptive thing is that Metz calls the product of his *techne* a "duplicate" of the natural object (the filmophanic film), and that he claims that the study of this "duplicate" will enable us to understand how films communicate.

However, a "duplicate" is a thing that exactly resembles another in appearance, pattern, or content. A "duplicate" is a copy. Metz provides no evidence whatsoever that his systems, structures, and activities between these systemic elements, which are creations of the analyst, are in any way related to the expressive elements of motion picture films. Also, he provides no evidence whatsoever from communication research or from any other source that the film audience engages in the kind of mental activities which he describes and which could explain how signification is achieved in films.

As for the manner in which the codes and sub-codes function to create the "cinematic language system," Metz provides no definite plan which sets the rules of behavior

161

of the various systemic elements which are involved. The activities of the various systemic elements appear to be made up by Metz as he goes along. The matter of the cinematic system becomes even more troublesome later on because Metz indicates that the system of each film is unique and unrepeatable. If that is the case, much of what he has said about systems cannot possibly be a blueprint for the cinematic systems in general which applies to all films.

Chapter III, "Metz and the Film Audience," examined Metz's approach in terms of that aspect of the reality of film which involves the audience's relationship with the filmophanic film.

In terms of the limitations of the phenomenological-structural linguistic aspects of Metz's work, in this chapter it was pointed out that Metz and the film audience are relating to two different things: Metz is relating to the "duplicate" product of his techne, and the audience is relating to the reality of film. Nothing that Metz proposes is in any way related to the emotional response involved in experiencing a film as projected in a motion picture theatre. He fails to examine the relationship between the audience and the signifier. He also fails to examine the relationship between the audience and anything even remotely associated with the connotation and the signified. The synchronic aspects of the structural linguistic approach trap Metz in such a way that he cannot account for any dimension of film which involves the diachronic aspects of the reality of film and of the experience of viewing films as they unfold diachronically.

As for the fact that film is an art form, Metz fails entirely to account for any aspect of the relationship between the audience and the filmophanic film which explains the manner in which human beings relate to a work of art. In describing the manner in which an analyst such as Metz relates to the mental "duplicate" of film, Metz also fails entirely to take into account that film is an art form. In *Film Language* and *Language and Cinema*, there is simply no analytic feature and no systemic relationship which in any way accounts for the analyst's relationship with any aspect of artistic inspiration, creation, or enjoyment.

In Chapter IV, "The Severed Roots," it was pointed out that Metz fails to deal with film as a cultural object functioning within the social process of communication.

Metz's exclusion of the sociocultural dimension of film was accomplished by not examining the role of visual perception in film communication, by excluding whatever may function as a cultural code, by failing to deal with socio-cultural influences in producing, exhibiting, and perceiving films, and in general by choosing to deal with film as a linguistic object rather than as an art form.

An important matter which this chapter also tried to point out is that as a film theorist Metz cannot function in a social vacuum. He must be approaching the study of film in terms of what is culturally meaningful to him. And yet, in *Film Language* and *Language and Cinema*, Metz makes no reference whatsoever to the sociocultural perspective from which an analyst like himself views and analyzes film, and he makes no provisions in his analytic procedures for such a viewpoint. The "duplicate" of the natural object is analyzed in an ideological and sociocultural vacuum.

In Chapter V, "The Imaginary Signifier," there is a brief description of Metz's new psychoanalytically inspired approach, certain comments on the relationship between his earlier phenomenological-linguistic approach and the new psychoanalytic approach, and an examination of the problems he encounters in terms of the new approach and the reality of film.

His new psychoanalytically inspired approach turns out to be not so new after all. The old phenomenological-structural linguistic approach, with all its weaknesses such as the impossible distinctions, the circularity of thought, the great vagueness and the impressionistic qualities, has been incorporated into the new approach. In this manner the ill-fated analogy that film is like a language is used now to support the new analogies that the unconscious mind is structured like a language and that film is like a dream.

These analogies, however, combined with Metz's lack of interest in the filmophanic film prevent him from focusing

on the object of his study and make the new approach as
impressionistic as the earlier one. The "film script"
which Metz intends to study psychoanalytically is a
confused and vague notion which becomes progressively even
more vague and confused as he attempts simultaneously to
enlarge and to limit it in a futile effort to bring it
under control. In this effort the "matter of the signifier"
remains hopelessly entangled in the very abstract distinctions "in Hjelmslev's sense." No attempt is made to
describe what is manifested in the "manifest filmic material," and how this manifestation comes about. The
"pertinent features" of the signifier are shrouded in
mystery.

His dependence on the ideas and writing style of Lacan
and on a view of Freudian psychoanalysis which, in its lack
of critical perspective, resembles the vulgarized interpre-
tations of Freud's work in popular magazines, introduce to
the linguistic-psychoanalytic approach a great lack of
precision and make it even more impressionistic than the
approach taken in *Language and Cinema*.

In terms of specific aspects of the reality of film,
in "The Imaginary Signifier" Metz employs some familiar
methods of acknowledging these aspects and then rejecting
them in the creation of the analytic procedures. The author
of the film is banished again with the excuse that dealing
with the author may lead to a "nosographic" or other type
of characterology. The content of film in terms of images

165

and sounds is rejected again. Despite the fact that he
uses the film/dream analogy which lends itself to a
psychoanalytic approach of film as an art form, Metz again
does not wish to deal with film as an art. He repeats in
"The Imaginary Signifier" the admission he made in *Film
Language* and *Language and Cinema* that film is a *hapax*. But,
just as he failed in his earlier approach to demonstrate how
the codes and sub-codes combine to produce the unique and
unrepeatable system of a film, in his new approach he fails
again to indicate how the codes (now re-named "codes of the
dream") combine to produce meaning and the unique quality of
a given film. Although the individual is viewed in psychoanalysis as a social being, and Freud analyzed artistic
activity in terms of its sociocultural dimension, Metz
attempts to use psychoanalytic concepts for the examination
of cinematic signification which ignore the sociocultural
roots of film.

In terms of the reality of film a very disturbing
aspect of his new approach is the handling of the matter of
spectator identification. According to Metz the spectator
identifies with the screen characters, the camera, the
screen, and with his own self. In examining this relationship Metz has an opportunity to make use of psychoanalysis
in order to deal with the reality of film. Instead, he
manipulates the psychoanalytic principles involved and the
concepts of linguistics which he has retained from the

earlier approach in order to retreat once more to the
abstract domain of structural linguistics. In this domain
the reality of film has no place. The only relationship
which is really examined is that between an analyst like
Metz and the analytic procedures which he invents for the
mental "duplicate" of the natural object.

Since the "duplicate" which he creates is not a
duplicate of film at all but an analytic entity for something which is not related to the reality of film, Metz's
entire effort represents a waste of time as far as helping
us understand how films communicate.

The study of Metz's "duplicate" seems to have some
value only in terms of the pleasure derived from manipulating a product of one's imagination which pulsates with that
special excitement which characterizes mental structures and
from sharing with others the experience involved in
constructing and manipulating such structures.

It seems to me quite possible that one could use the
Metz "method" to fill thousands of pages with equally
fascinating mental acrobatics describing the transformations
and contaminations of codes, sub-codes, and systems without
reference to film or anything else of any specific nature.
The question is, Why does Metz involve the cinema in such a
tortuous and unproductive enterprise? It is conceivable the
answer lies in that, despite his repeated professions of
great love for the cinema, Metz may not have real respect

and affection for the seventh and liveliest art. Before attempting to analyze his written treatises on film, perhaps one should pressure Metz to elaborate a little more on a statement which he made once in response to questions put to him by *Cinéthique*. Said Metz:

> I do not consider the film-maker as a creative individual at all.[1]

FOOTNOTES

[1]*Cinéthique,* "On *Langage et Cinéma,*" p. 209.

BIBLIOGRAPHY

BIBLIOGRAPHY

Altaman, Charles F. "Psychoanalysis and Cinema: The Imag-
    inary Discourse." *Quarterly Review of Film Studies,* 2
    No. 1, August, 1977, 257-272.

Andrew, Dudley J. *The Major Film Theories: An Introduction.*
    Oxford: Oxford University Press, 1976.

_____. "Film Analysis or Film Therapy: To Step
    Beyond Semiotics." *Quarterly Review of Film Studies,* 2,
    No. 1, February, 1977, 33-41.

Barthes, Roland. *Elements of Semiology.* London: Jonathan
    Cape, 1969.

Baudry, Jean-Louis. "Ideological Effects of the Basic
    Cinematographic Apparatus." *Film Quarterly,* 28, No. 2,
    Winter, 1974/75, 39-47.

Bauxandall, Lee. *Marxism and Aesthetics: A Selective Annotated
    Bibliography; Books and Articles in the English Language.* New
    York: Humanities Press, 1968.

Bellour, Raymond. "The Obvious and the Code." *Screen,* 15,
    No. 4, Winter, 1974/75, 7-17.

Benoist, Jean-Marie. "Structuralism: A New Frontier."
    Cambridge Review, 93, No. 2204, October 22, 1971, 10-17.

Bettetini, Gianfranco. *The Language and Technique of the Film.*
    The Hague: Mouton, 1973.

Bizet, Jacques-Andre. "Les Structuralistes, la Notion de
    Structure et l'Esthetique du Film." *La Pensèe,* 137,
    February, 1968, 38-50.

Bochenski, I. M. *The Methods of Contemporary Thought.* Dordrecht,
    Holland: D. Reidel Publishing Co., 1965.

Boon, James A. *From Symbolism to Structuralism: Lévi-Strauss in a
    Literary Tradition.* Oxford: Blackwell, 1972.

Bowlt, John. "Russian Formalism and the Visual Arts." *20th*

Century Studies, 7/8, December, 1972, 131-146.

Brewster, Ben. "Structuralism in Film Criticism." *Screen*, 12, No. 1, Spring, 1971, 49-58.

Broekman, Jan M. *Structuralism: Moscow, Prague, Paris*. Boston: D. Reidel Publishing Co., 1974.

Burch, Noel. *Theory of Film Practice*. New York: Praeger, 1973.

Buscombe, Edward, and others. "Ideas of Authorship." *Screen*, 14, No. 3, Autumn, 1973, 75-85.

_____, and others. "Psychoanalysis and Film." *Screen*, 16, No. 4, Winter, 1975/76, 119-130.

_____, and others. "Why We Have Resigned from the Board of *Screen*." *Screen*, 17, no. 2, Summer, 1976, 106-109.

Casey, John. *The Language of Criticism*. London: Methuen, 1966.

Cegarra, Michel. "Cinema and Semiology." *Screen*, 14, No. 1/2, Spring/Summer, 1973, 129-188.

Chatman, Seymour. "Discussion of Gilbert Harman's Paper, 'Semiotics and the Cinema.'" *Quarterly Review of Film Studies*, 2, No. 1, February, 1977, 25-32.

Cinéthique. "On *Langage et Cinéma*." *Screen*, 14, no. 1/2, Spring/Summer, 1973, 189-213.

Comolli, J. L., and Narboni, J. "Cinema/Ideology/Criticism: Examining a Critique at Its Critical Point." *Screen*, 13, No. 1 Spring, 1972, 120-131.

Cornforth, Maurice C. *Marxism and the Linguistic Philosophy*. New York: International Publishers, 1966.

Crystal, David. *Linguistics*. Harmondsworth: Penguin, 1971.

Culler, Jonathan D. *Structuralist Poetics: Structuralism, Linguistics, and the Study of Literature*. London: Routledge & Kegan Paul, 1975.

Daniel, Jack. "Metz's *Grande Syntagmatique:* Summary and Critique." *Film Form*, 1, No. 1, Spring, 1976, 78-90.

DeGeorge, Richard T., and Fernande, M., Eds. *The Structuralists from Marx to Lévi-Strauss*. Garden City, N. Y.: Anchor Books, 1972.

Dembo, L. S., Ed. *Criticism; Speculative and Analytical Essays.* Maddison, Milwaukee: The University of Wisconsin Press, 1968.

Eckert, Charles W. "The English Cine-Structuralists." *Film Comment,* 9, No. 3, May-June, 1973, 46-51.

Eco, Umberto. "On the Contribution of Film to Semiotics." *Quarterly Review of Film Studies,* 2, No. 1, February, 1977, 1-14.

_____. *A Theory of Semiotics.* Bloomington: Indiana University Press, 1976.

Ehrenzweig, Anton. *The Psychoanalysis of Artistic Vision and Hearing.* New York: George Braziller, 1965.

Ehrmann, Jacques. *Structuralism.* Garden City, N. Y.: Doubleday & Co., 1970.

Eikhenbaum, Boris. "Problems of Film Stylistics." *Screen,* 15, No. 3, Autumn, 1974, 7-34.

Erickson, Stephen A. *Language and Being: An Analytic Phenomenology.* New Haven: Yale University Press, 1970.

Feibleman, James Kern. *Scientific Method.* The Hague: Nijhoff, 1972.

Fieandt, Kai von. *The World of Perception.* Homewood, Illinois: The Dorsey Press, 1966.

Fischer, Ernst. *Art Against Ideology.* London: Penguin Books, 1969.

Fraiberg, Louis. *Psychoanalysis and American Literary Criticism.* Detroit: Wayne State University Press, 1960.

Freud, Sigmund. *The Ego and the Id.* London: Hogwarth Press, 1947.

_____. *Beyond the Pleasure Principle.* London: Hogwarth Press, 1948.

_____. *An Outline of Psychoanalysis.* New York: W. W. Norton & Co., 1949.

_____. *Collected Papers.* 4 vols. London: Hogwarth Press, 1950.

_____. *The Interpretation of Dreams.* London: Hogwarth Press, 1953.

Frondizi, Risieri. *What Is Value? An Introduction to Axiology.* LaSalle, Illinois: Open Court Publishing Co., 1971.

Fyock, James A. "Content Analysis of Films: New Slant of an Old Technique." *Journalism Quarterly,* 35, No. 4, 1968, 687-691.

Gardies, Renè. "Structural Analysis of a Textual System: Presentation of a Method." *Screen,* 15, No. 1, Spring, 1974, 11-32.

Glucksman, Miriam. *Structural Analysis in Contemporary Social Thought; A Comparison of the Theories of Claude Lévi-Strauss and Louis Althusser.* London: Routledge & K. Paul, 1974.

Graff, Gerald. "What Was New Criticism? Literary Interpretation and Scientific Objectivity." *Salmagundi,* 27, Summer-Fall, 1974, 72-93.

Guzzetti, Alfred. "Christian Metz and the Semiology of the Cinema." *Journal of Modern Literature,* 3, No. 2, April, 1973, 272-308.

Hall, Calvin S. *A Primer of Freudian Psychology.* New York: The World Publishing Co., 1963.

Handy, Rollo. *Methodology of the Behavioral Sciences.* Springfield, Illinois: Charles C. Thomas Publisher, 1964.

Handy, William J., ed. *A Symposium on Formalist Criticism.* Austin, Texas: The University of Texas Press, 1965.

Harman, Gilbert. "Semiotics and the Cinema: Metz and Wollen." *Quarterly Review of Film Studies,* 2, No. 1, February, 1977, 15-24.

Harpole, Charles, and Hanhardt, John. "Linguistics, Structuralism, Semiology: Approaches to Cinema with a Bibliography." *Film Comment,* 9, No. 3, May-June, 1973, 52-59.

Harré, R. *An Introduction to the Logic of the Sciences.* London: MacMillan & Co., 1960.

Harris, Marvin. *The Rise of Anthropological Theory: A History of Theories of Culture.* New York: Thomas Crowell Co., 1968.

Hartmann, Reinhard. *The Language of Linguistics: Reflections on Linguistic Terminology.* Tübingen: Tübingen Beiträge zur Linguistik, 1973.

Hayes, E. Nelson, and Hayes, Tanya, eds. *Claude Lévi-Strauss: The Anthropologist as Hero.* Cambridge: Massachusetts Institute of Technology Press, 1970.

Heath, Stephen. "Film/Cinetext/Text." *Screen,* 14, No. 1/2, Spring/Summer, 1973, 102-128.

_____. "Metz's Semiology: A Short Glossary." *Screen,* 14, No. 1/2, Spring/Summer, 1973, 214-226.

_____. "Comments on 'The Idea of Authorship.'" *Screen,* 14, No. 3, Autumn, 1973, 86-91.

_____. "The Work of Christian Metz." *Screen,* 14, No. 3, Autumn, 1973, 5-28.

_____. "Film and System, Terms of Analysis, Part I." *Screen,* 16, No. 1, Spring, 1975, 7-77.

_____. "Film and System, Terms of Analysis, Part II." *Screen,* 16, No. 2, Summer, 1975, 91-113.

Heaton, J. M. "Insight in Phenomenology and Psychoanalysis." *Journal of the British Society for Phenomenology,* 3, No. 2, May, 1972, 135-145.

Heller, Louis G., and Macris, James. *Toward a Structural Theory of Literary Analysis; Prolegomena to Evaluative Descriptivism.* Worcester: Massachusetts Institute for Systems Analysis, 1970.

Henderson, Brian. "Toward a Non-Bourgeois Camera Style." *Film Quarterly,* 24, No. 2, Winter, 1970-71, 2-14.

_____. "Two Types of Film Theory." *Film Quarterly,* 24, No. 3, Spring, 1971, 33-41.

_____. "Metz: 'Essais I' and Film Theory." *Film Quarterly,* 28, No. 3, Spring, 1975, 12-33.

Hendricks, William O. *Essays on Semiolinguistics and Verbal Art.* The Hague: Mouton, 1973.

Hill, Anthony. "A Structuralist Art?" *20th Century Studies,* 3, May, 1970, 102-109.

Hirsch, E. D. *Validity in Interpretation.* New Haven: Yale University Press, 1967.

Hjelmslev, Louis. *Prolegomena to a Theory of Language.* Madison, Milwaukee: The University of Wisconsin Press, 1963.

Hjelmslev, Louis. *Language: An Introduction*. Madison, Milwaukee: The University of Wisconsin Press, 1970.

Hobsbaum, Philip. *Theory of Criticism*. Bloomington: Indiana University Press, 1970.

Hogg, James, ed. *Psychology of the Visual Arts*. Baltimore: Penguin Books, 1969.

Ihde, Don. *Hermeneutic Phenomenology*. Evanston: Northwestern University Press, 1971.

Jacobson, Roman, and Hale, Morris. *Fundamentals of Language*. The Hague: Mouton, 1956.

Jameson, Fredric. *Marxism and Form: Twentieth-Century Dialectical Theories of Criticism*. Princeton: Princeton University Press, 1972.

_____. *The Prison-House of Language: A Critical Account of Structuralism and Russian Formalism*. Princeton, New Jersey: Princeton University Press, 1972.

Jarvie, I. C. *Movies and Society*. New York: Basic Books, Inc., 1970.

Jean, B., and Lewis, T. J. "Structural Linguistics and Literature in France." *Journal of the British Society for Phenomenology*, 2, No. 3, October, 1971, 27-36.

Kitses, Jim. *Horizons West*. Bloomington: Indiana University Press, 1969.

Klein, Melanie. *Psychoanalysis of Children*. London: Hogwarth Press, 1933.

_____. *Contribution to Psychoanalysis, 1921-1945*. London: Hogwarth Press, 1948.

_____. *Envy and Gratitude*. New York: Basic Books, Inc., 1957.

Kristeva, Julia. "The Semiotic Activity." *Screen*, 14, No. 1/2, Summer, 1973, 25-39.

Kroeber, A. L. *Culture: A Critical Review of Concepts and Definitions*. New York: Peabody Museum of American Archaeology, 1952.

Kuntzel, Thiery. "The Treatment of Ideology in the Textual Analysis of Film." *Screen*, 14, No. 3, Autumn, 1973, 44-54.

Lacan, Jacques. "Some Reflections on the Ego." *International Journal of Psycho-Analysis,* 34, 1953, 11-17.

_____. *Ecrits.* Paris: Seuil, 1966.

_____. *The Language of the Self: The Function of Language in Psychoanalysis.* Baltimore: The Johns Hopkins Press, 1968.

_____. "The Mirror-Phase." *New Left Review,* 51, 1968, 71-77.

_____. "On Structure As an Inmixing of an Otherness Prerequisite to Any Subject Whatever." *The Languages of Criticism and the Sciences of Man: The Structuralist Controversy,* eds. R. Macksey and E. Donato. Baltimore: Johns Hopkins Press, 1970, 186-200.

_____. *Les Quatre Concepts Fondamentaux de la Psychanalyse.* Paris: Seuil, 1973.

Lane, Michael, ed. *Structuralism: A Reader.* London: Jonathan Cape, 1970.

Leach, Edmund. *Lévi-Strauss.* London: William Collins & Co., 1970.

Lepley, Ray, ed. *The Language of Value.* New York: Columbia University Press, 1957.

Lepschy, Giulio C. *A Survey of Structural Linguistics.* London: Faber, 1970.

LeSage, Laurent. *The French New Criticism.* University Park: The Pennsylvania State University Press, 1967.

LeSage, Julia. "The Human Subject--You, He, or Me?" *Screen,* 16, No. 2, Summer, 1975, 77-82.

Lévi-Strauss, Claude. *Structural Anthropology.* New York: Basic Books, Inc., 1963.

_____. *The Elementary Structures of Kinship.* London: Eyre & Spottiswood, 1969.

Lovell, Alan. "Notes on British Film Culture." *Screen,* 13, No. 2, Summer, 1972, 5-16.

_____. "Robin Wood--A Dissenting View." *Screen,* 10, No. 2, March/April, 1969, 42-55.

Lovell, Terry. "Cultural Studies." *Screen,* 14, No. 3,

Autumn, 1973, 115-122.

Lyas, Colin, ed. *Philosophy and Linguistics*. London: Macmillan & Co., 1971.

MacBean, James Roy. "Godard's 'Weekend,' or the Self-Critical Cinema of Cruelty." *Film Quarterly*, 21, No. 2, Winter, 1968-1969, 35-43.

_____. "Politics, Painting, and the Language of Signs in Godard's 'Made in U.S.A.'" *Film Quarterly*, 22, No. 3, Spring, 1969, 18-25.

_____. "See You at Mao." *Film Quarterly*, 24, No. 2, Winter, 1970-1971, 15-23.

_____. *Film and Revolution*. Bloomington: Indiana University Press, 1975.

Macksey, Richard, and Donato, Eugenio, eds. *The Languages of Criticism and the Sciences of Man: The Structuralist Controversy*. Baltimore: The Johns Hopkins Press, 1970.

Matejka, Ladislav, and Titunik, Irwin, eds. *Semiotics of Art: Prague School Contributions*. Cambridge, Mass.: Massachusetts Institute of Technology Press, 1976.

Metz, Christian. *Essais sur la signification au Cinéma*. Paris: Editions Klincksieck, 1968.

_____. *Langage et Cinéma*. Paris: Larousse, 1971.

_____. "Jean Mitry's 'L'Esthétique et Psychologie du Cinéma.'" *Screen*, 14, No. 1/2, Spring/Summer, 1973, 40-88.

_____. "Methodological Propositions for the Analysis of Film." *Screen*, 14, No. 1/2, Spring,Summer, 1973, 89-101.

_____. *Film Language: A Semiotics of the Cinema*. New York: Oxford University Press, 1974.

_____. *Language and Cinema*. The Hague: Mouton, 1974.

_____. "The Imaginary Signifier." *Screen*, 16, No. 2, Summer, 1975, 14-76.

_____. "L'incandescence et le code." *Cahiers du Cinéma*, 274, March, 1977, 5-22.

Miel, Jan. *Jacques Lacan and the Structure of the Unconscious.*
Yale French Studies, Nos. 36-37. New Haven: Yale
University Press, 1966, 104-111.

Moles, Abraham. *Information Theory and Esthetic Perception.*
Urbana: The University of Illinois Press, 1966.

Monaco, James. *How to Read a Film.* New York: Oxford University Press, 1977.

Morick, Harold, ed. *Wittgenstein and the Problem of Other Minds.*
New York: McGraw-Hill, 1967.

Morris, Charles. *Signification and Significance: A Study of the
Relations of Signs and Values.* Cambridge: Massachusetts
Institute of Technology Press, 1970.

_____. *Writings on the General Theory of Signs.* The
Hague: Mouton, 1971.

Morse, David. "Criticism As a Science." *20th Century Studies,*
9, September, 1973, 32-50.

Mullahy, Patrick. *Oedipus Myth and Complex.* New York: Hermit-
age House, 1949.

Murray, John C. "Robin Wood and the Structural Critics."
Screen, 12, No. 3, Summer, 1971, 101-110.

Najder, Zdzislaw. *Values and Evaluations.* Oxford: Clarendon
Press, 1975.

Nowell-Smith, Geoffrey. "Cinema and Structuralism," *20th
Century Studies,* 3, May, 1970, 131-139.

_____. "I Was a Star-Struck Structural-
ist." *Screen,* 14, No. 3, Autumn, 1973, 92-100.

Pasquier, Sylvain du. "Buster Keaton's Gags." *Journal of
Modern Literature,* 3, No. 2, April, 1973, 269-291.

Pettit, Philip. "Wittgenstein and the Case for Structuralism." *Journal of the British Society for Phenomenology,* 3,
No. 1, January, 1972, 46-57.

_____. *The Concept of Structuralism: A Critical Analysis.*
Berkeley: University of California Press, 1975.

Petrie, Graham. "Auteurism: More Aftermath." *Film Quarterly,*
27, No. 3, Spring, 1974, 61-62.

Piaget, Jean. *Structuralism*. New York: Basic Books, 1970.

Poirier, Richard. *The Performing Self: Compositions and Decompositions in the Languages of Contemporary Life*. New York: Oxford University Press, 1971.

Pool, Roger C. "Structuralism and Phenomenology: A Literary Approach." *Journal of the British Society for Phenomenology*, 2, No. 2, May, 1971, 3-16.

Pryluck, Calvin. "Toward a Psycholinguistics of Cinema." *AV Communication Review*, 15, No. 1, Spring, 1967, 54-75.

_____. "Structural Analysis of Motion Pictures As a Symbol System." *AV Communication Review*, 16, No. 4, Winter, 1968, 372-402.

_____. "Motion Pictures and Language: A Comparative Analysis." *Journal of the University Film Association*, 21, No. 2, 1969, 46-51.

_____. "The Film Metaphor-Metaphor: The Use of Language-Based Models in Film Study." *Film Literature Quarterly*, 3, No. 2, Spring, 1975, 117-123.

Richards, I. A. *Principles of Literary Criticism*. New York: Harcourt, Brace & Co., 1950.

Rifflet-Lemaire, A. *Jacques Lacan*. Brussels: Dessart, 1970.

Riley, Gresham, ed. *Values, Objectivity and the Social Sciences*. Reading, Mass.: Addison-Wesley Pub. Co., 1974.

Robey, David. *Structuralism: An Introduction*. Oxford: Clarendon Press, 1973.

Rohdie, Sam. "Movie Reader, Film As Film." *Screen*, 13, No. 4, Winter, 1972/73, 135-145.

Ross, S. D. *The Scientific Process*. The Hague: Martinus Nijhoff, 1971.

Rossi, Ino, ed. *The Unconscious in Culture: The Structuralism of Claude Lévi-Strauss in Perspective*. New York: E. P. Dutton & Co., 1974.

Salt, Barry. "Statistical Style Analysis of Motion Pictures." *Film Quarterly*, 28, No. 1, Fall, 1974, 13-21.

Sarris, Andrew. "Where I Stand on the New Film-Crit." *The Village Voice*, 20, No. 32, August 11, 1975.

Saussure, Ferdinand de. *Course in General Linguistics*. London: Peter Owen, 1960.

Scheffler, Israel. *Science and Subjectivity*. New York: Bobbs-Merrill & Co., 1967.

Schilder, Paul. *Psychoanalysis, Man, and Society*. New York: W. W. Norton & Co., 1951.

Scholes, Robert. *Structuralism in Literature*. New Haven: Yale University Press, 1974.

Sebag, Lucien. *Marxisme et structuralism*. Paris: Payot, 1964.

Segal, Hanna. *Introduction to the Work of Melanie Klein*. New York: Basic Books, 1964.

Segre, Cesare. *Semiotics and Literary Criticism*. The Hague: Mouton, 1973.

_____. "Space and Time of the Text." *20th Century Studies*, 12, December, 1974, 37-41.

Shands, Harley C. "Semiotics Approaches to Psychiatry." *Approaches to Semiotics*, ed. T. A. Sebeok. The Hague: Mouton, 1970.

Sieminska, Ewa. "Connotation and Denotation in a Work of Film Art." *Sign, Language, Culture*, ed. A. J. Greimas. The Hague: Mouton, 1970.

Silverstein, Norman. "American Film Reviewers and French Critics." *Salmagundi*, 14, Fall, 1970, 105-112.

Simon, Julian L. *Basic Research Methods in Social Science: The Art of Empirical Investigation*. New York: Random House, 1969.

Smith, Alfred, ed. *Communication and Culture: Readings in the Codes of Human Interaction*. New York: Holt, Rinehart & Winston, 1966.

Todorov, Tzvetan. *Littérature et Signification*. Paris: Larousse, 1967.

_____. "Freud sur l'énonciation." *Languages*, 5, March, 1970, 34-41.

_____. "Some Approaches to Russian Formalism." *20th Century Studies*, 7/8, December, 1972, 6-19.

_____. "Semiotics." *Screen*, 14, No. 1/2, Spring/Summer, 1973, 15-24.

Tudor, Andrew. *Image and Influence: Studies in the Sociology of Film.* London: Allen & Unwin, 1974.

_____. *Theories of Film.* London: Secker & Warburg, 1974.

Uitti, Karl D. *Linguistics and Literary Theory.* New York: Norton & Co., 1974.

Viet, Jean. *Les Méthodes Structuralistes dans les Sciences Sociales.* La Haye: Mouton, 1969.

Vogel, Amos. "The Structuralist Incursion." *Film Comment,* 2, No. 4, July-August, 1975, 37.

Waugh, Butler. "Structural Analysis in Literature and Folklore." *Western Folklore,* 25, 1966, 153-164.

Weber, Max. *The Methodology of the Social Sciences.* Glencoe, Illinois: The Free Press, 1949.

Wellek, R. *Concepts of Criticism.* New Haven: Yale University Press, 1963.

_____. *The Literary Theory and Aesthetics of the Prague School.* Ann Arbor: The University of Michigan Press, 1969.

_____. *Discriminations.* New Haven: Yale University Press, 1970.

Wetherill, P. M. *The Literary Text: An Examination of Critical Methods.* Oxford: Basil Blackwell, 1974.

"Why We Have Resigned from the Board of *Screen.*" *Screen,* 17, No. 2, Summer, 1976, 106-109.

Willemen, Paul. "Reflections on Eikhenbaum's Concept of Internal Speech in the Cinema." *Screen,* 15, No. 4, Winter, 1974/75, 59-70.

Williams, Alan. "Structures of Narrativity in Fritz Lang's 'Metropolis.'" *Film Quarterly,* 27, No. 4, Summer, 1974, 17-23.

Whitney, Edward, ed. *Symbology: The Use of Symbols in Visual Communication.* New York: Hastings House, 1960.

Wilden, Anthony. "Freud, Signorelli, and Lacan: The Repression of the Signifier." *American Imago,* 23, No. 4, Winter, 1966, 332-366.

_____. "Jacques Lacan: A Partial Bibliography."

182

Yale French Studies, 36-37, October, 1966, 263-268.

Wilden, Anthony. *System and Structure: Essays in Communication and Exchange.* London: Tavistock Publications, 1972.

Wolff, Janet. *Hermeneutic Philosophy and the Sociology of Art.* London: Routledge & Paul, 1975.

Wollen, Peter, ed. *Working Papers on the Cinema: Sociology and Semiology.* London: British Film Institute, 1968.

_____. *Signs and Meaning in the Cinema.* Blooming-ton: Indiana University Press, 1972.

_____. "Structuralism Implies a Certain Kind of Methodology." *Film Heritage,* Summer, 1974, 21-29.

Wood, Robin. "Ghostly Paradigm and H. C. F.: An Answer to Alan Lovell." *Screen,* 10, No. 3, May/June, 1969, 35-48.

_____. "Art and Ideology: Notes on 'Silk Stockings.'" *Film Comment,* 11, No. 3, May-June, 1975, 28-31.

_____. "In Defense of Art." *Film Comment,* 11, No. 4, July-August, 1975, 44-51.

_____. "Against Conclusions." *Film Comment,* 11, No. 5, September-October, 1975, 30-32.

_____. "Old Wine, New Battles: Structuralism or Humanism?" *Film Comment,* 12, No. 6, November-December, 1976, 22-25.

Worth, Sol. "The Development of a Semiotic of Film." *Semiotica,* 13, 1969, 282-321.

Wright, Will. *Six Guns and Society: A Structural Study of the Western.* Berkeley: University of California Press, 1975.

Youngren, William H. *Semantics, Linguistics, and Criticism.* New York: Random House, 1972.

DISSERTATIONS ON FILM 1980

An Arno Press Collection

Allen, Robert C. **Vaudeville and Film 1895-1915: A Study in Media Interaction** (Doctoral Dissertation, The University of Iowa, 1977). 1980

Bordwell, David. **French Impressionist Cinema: Film Culture, Film Theory, and Film Style** (Doctoral Dissertation, The University of Iowa, 1974). 1980

Brown, Kent R. **The Screenwriter as Collaborator: The Career of Stewart Stern** (Doctoral Dissertation, The University of Iowa, 1972). 1980 ₄

Cozyris, George Agis. **Christian Metz and the Reality of Film** (Doctoral Dissertation, The University of Southern California, 1979). 1980

Curran, Trisha. **A New Note on the Film: A Theory of Film Criticism Derived from Susanne K. Langer's Philosophy of Art** (Doctoral Dissertation, Ohio State University, 1978). 1980

Daly, David Anthony. **A Comparison of Exhibition and Distribution Patterns in Three Recent Feature Motion Pictures** (Doctoral Dissertation, Southern Illinois University, 1978). 1980

Diakité, Madubuko. **Film, Culture, and the Black Filmmaker: A Study of Functional Relationships and Parallel Developments** (Doctoral Dissertation, Stockholm University, 1978). 1980

Editors of *Look*. **Movie Lot to Beachhead: The Motion Picture Goes to War and Prepares for the Future.** 1945

Ellis, Reed. **A Journey Into Darkness: The Art of James Whale's Horror Films** (Doctoral Dissertation, The University of Florida, 1979). 1980

Fleener-Marzec, Nickieann. **D.W. Griffith's** *The Birth of a Nation*: **Controversy, Suppression, and the First Amendment as it Applies to Filmic Expression, 1915-1973** (Doctoral Dissertation, The University of Wisconsin, 1977). 1980

Garton, Joseph W. **The Film Acting of John Barrymore** (Doctoral Dissertation, New York University, 1977). 1980

Gehring, Wes D. **Leo McCarey and the Comic Anti-Hero in American Film** (Doctoral Dissertation, The University of Iowa, 1977). 1980

Kindem, Gorham Anders. **Toward a Semiotic Theory of Visual Communication in the Cinema: A Reappraisal of Semiotic Theories from a Cinematic Perspective and a Semiotic Analysis of Color Signs and Communication in the Color Films of Alfred Hitchcock** (Doctoral Dissertation, Northwestern University, 1977). 1980

Manvell, Roger. **Ingmar Bergman: An Appreciation.** 1980

Moore, Barry Walter. **Aesthetic Aspects of Recent Experimental Film** (Doctoral Dissertation, The University of Michigan, 1977). 1980

Nichols, William James. **Newsreel: Documentary Filmmaking on the American Left** (Doctoral Dissertation, The University of California, Los Angeles, 1975). 1980

Rose, Brian Geoffrey. **An Examination of Narrative Structure in Four Films of Frank Capra** (Doctoral Dissertation, The University of Wisconsin, 1976). 1980

Salvaggio, Jerry Lee. **A Theory of Film Language** (Doctoral Dissertation, The University of Michigan, 1978). 1980

Simonet, Thomas Solon. **Regression Analysis of Prior Experiences of Key Production Personnel as Predictors of Revenues from High-Grossing Motion Pictures in American Release** (Doctoral Dissertation, Temple University, 1977). 1980

Siska, William Charles. **Modernism in the Narrative Cinema: The Art Film as a Genre** (Doctoral Dissertation, Northwestern University, 1976). 1980

Stewart, Lucy Ann Liggett. **Ida Lupino as Film Director, 1949-1953: An Auteur Approach** (Doctoral Dissertation, The University of Michigan, 1979). 1980

Strebel, Elizabeth Grottle. **French Social Cinema of the Nineteen Thirties: A Cinematographic Expression of Popular Front Consciousness** (Doctoral Dissertation, Princeton University, 1973). 1980

Veeder, Gerry K. **The Influence of Subliminal Suggestion on the Response to Two Films** (Doctoral Dissertation, Wayne State University, 1975). 1980

Vincent, Richard C. **Financial Characteristics of Selected 'B' Film Productions of Albert J. Cohen, 1951-1957** (Masters Thesis, Temple University, 1977). 1980

Williams, Alan Larson. **Max Ophuls and the Cinema of Desire** (Doctoral Dissertation, The State University of New York, Buffalo, 1977). 1980